HUMAN RESOURCE DEVELOPMENT in RURAL TEXAS

Studies in Human Resource Development No. 1

HUMAN RESOURCE DEVELOPMENT in RURAL TEXAS

Ray Marshall, James L. Walker,
and R. Lynn Rittenoure

A Joint Publication
of the
Center for the Study of Human Resources
and the
Bureau of Business Research
of
The University of Texas at Austin

Library of Congress Catalog Card Number: 74-12528

ISBN 87755-198-7

1974 $4.00

CONTENTS

LIST OF TABLES

Manpower Appendix

Statistical Appendix

PUBLISHER'S FOREWORD

The Bureau of Business Research is pleased to cooperate with the Center for the Study of Human Resources in the joint publication of a new series, Studies in Human Resource Development. The first volume in this series, *Human Resource Development in Rural Texas*, by Ray Marshall, R. Lynn Rittenoure, and James L. Walker, explores the extent of unemployment and poverty in rural Texas, evaluates human resource development programs designed to alleviate these problems, and recommends methods for strengthening the programs.

Ray Marshall is professor of economics and director of the Center for the Study of Human Resources at The University of Texas at Austin. He is president of the Southern Economic Association (1973-74), director of the Task Force on Southern Rural Development of the Southern Regional Council, and serves as a member of the National Manpower Policy Task Force, the National Manpower Advisory Committee, and the consortium on Rural Manpower Development of the U.S. Department of Labor. He has written a wide variety of books and articles in the fields of labor economics, manpower, and rural development, including *Rural Workers in Rural Labor Markets* (Salt Lake City: Olympus Publishing Company, 1974), *Human Resources and Labor Markets* (with Sar Levitan and Garth Mangum, New York: Harper and Row, 1972), and *Cooperatives and Rural Poverty in the South* (with Lamond Godwin, Baltimore: Johns Hopkins Press, 1971).

R. Lynn Rittenoure and James L. Walker both received doctorates in economics from The University of Texas at Austin and were research associates in the Center for the Study of Human Resources at the time *Human Resource Development in Rural*

Texas was written. Rittenoure's study of public employment in the rural south will be published as No. 3 in the Studies in Human Resource Development series. He is currently assistant professor of economics at the Naval Postgraduate School in Monterey, California. Walker, who has studied patterns of rural industrialization, is assistant professor of economics at the University of North Carolina in Greensboro.

Human Resource Development in Rural Texas was edited and prepared for publication by Kathleen Luft and Margaret Woodruff. The cover was designed by William Hezlep. Compositors were Jennifer Brewster, Sandy Kessler, and Clintsy Sturgill. Offset printing was done by Robert Dorsett and Daniel P. Rosas, with the assistance of Robert Jenkins and Salvador Macias.

Stanley A. Arbingast
Director

July 1974

ACKNOWLEDGMENTS

We wish to thank the many persons who were of assistance to us in writing this book. James Webb and Roy Van Cleve, whose papers are contained in the appendix, had substantial influence on the text. In addition, Curtis Toews, Robert Glover, and Dann Milne offered valuable criticism and suggestions on earlier drafts of the study.

Our sincere thanks goes to those who worked with us. Jack Whiting, Tom Freeland, and Robert Wells designed and ran the computer programs to produce much of the data used in the study. In this effort, Sharla Walker and Susie Stanbery assisted with the coding. Susie Turner and Margo Pluta typed the manuscript. Kathleen Luft improved the manuscript considerably with her editorial changes. Finally, we are most appreciative for the assistance and encouragement provided to us by Stanley Arbingast of the Bureau of Business Research.

Human Resource Development in Rural Texas was prepared under financing from the Texas Rural Development Commission, with the helpful cooperation of its chairperson, Ray Prewett. Members of the commission's Human Resources Committee—Mike Burkholder, chairperson, Marie Burton, Joe E. Chapa, Jim Copp, Bill Daniels, John Hutchison, Dolphus Jones, Robert J. Mullins, James Powell, Zook Thomas, and Murray Travis—also provided valuable input to the study.

Ray Marshall
R. Lynn Rittenoure
James L. Walker

July 1974

PREFACE

Organizationally this report follows quite closely questions posed in discussions with the Human Resources Committee (HRC) of the Texas Rural Development Commission during 1972. The report is aimed at assisting the committee with its expressed goal, "To evaluate the extent and severity of poverty in rural Texas and to develop strategies for alleviating unemployment, underemployment, and low incomes."[1]

It was originally intended that the report would rely mainly on secondary sources. However, available information was found grossly inadequate. It therefore was necessary to generate, by sampling procedures, additional statistical information that was not readily available. Some of these data are included in the statistical appendix.

Several researchers also undertook extensive interviews to secure information about the operation of some of the more important human resource development programs in rural Texas. Separate reports on four of those programs are included in an appendix. Finally, the authors developed a regression model to quantify the relationship of various factors to economic growth. This model and the results derived from it are included in the statistical appendix, but relevant conclusions are stated at various places in the body of the report.

Much misunderstanding is caused by difficulties involved in defining "rural," a problem complicated by the fact that government agencies define the term in different ways. For example, the

---

[1]Human Resources Committee, Texas Rural Development Commission, statement, June 27, 1972.

Bureau of the Census defines as rural a place with fewer than 2,500 people, while the U.S. Department of Labor (DOL) defines as rural those counties where a majority of the people live in places with populations below 2,500. Thus the DOL definition would include people living in places larger than 2,500 if those places were in counties where a majority of the people lived in places with populations under 2,500. The DOL definition therefore places a smaller proportion of the nation's population in the rural category than the census definition. The Texas Communities Tomorrow program adopted in 1969 was aimed at communities of less than 12,000 population. The federal Rural Development Act of 1972 added two new definitions. For most purposes, rural places are defined as places with fewer than 10,000 people. However, business loans and grants are available for places of 50,000 and below (with population densities of less than 100 people per square mile). In general, the act gives priority to places with population below 25,000.

Sometimes data are reported on a metropolitan or nonmetropolitan basis. SMSAs, or "Standard Metropolitan Statistical Areas," are generally defined as a county or group of counties containing at least one city or combination of cities of 50,000 or more. When such data are used, rural and nonmetropolitan become interchangeable terms. This definition, however, often creates confusion when used as a substitute for "rural," because it encompasses larger areas than the census definition. In 1970, for example, only about 60 percent of Texas' nonmetropolitan population was classified as rural by the census definition.

Definitions are important because they influence our ability to understand what is happening in various areas. For example, it means little that the incidence of poverty is higher in rural areas or that rural populations are fairly constant unless we know what we mean by rural. Unfortunately, however, we are unable to resolve the confusion on this question and must therefore rely primarily on the form in which the data are presented by the primary sources. We believe, however, that the Rural Development Act's definition is more appropriate for developmental purposes than that of either the Bureau of the Census or the U.S. Department of Labor, because it facilitates the coordination of distant rural counties with larger towns and cities within an area.

As used in this report, "human resource development" includes (1) economic development (job creation); (2) education; (3) manpower; (4) antidiscrimination programs; and (5) health, welfare, and income maintenance activities. All of these activities clearly should be interrelated. Manpower training, for example, means little if jobs are not available. On the other hand, experience indicates that high-wage-growth industries are attracted by an assured supply of trained workers, so manpower training can be a significant inducement to industry.

Of all the components of human resource development activities, manpower programs probably are the least understood, partly because this area is relatively new, having grown significantly during the 1960s as a result of the Manpower Development and Training Act of 1962 and the Economic Opportunity Act of 1964. To avoid confusion, the following discrete functional elements are included in our definition of manpower programs:

1. Training, whether institutional (classroom), on-the-job (OJT), or some combination of these (as in apprenticeship programs), which seeks to enhance trainees' employability and income by adding to their skills.

2. Public employment programs, which create jobs in the public sector for designated groups, such as unemployed veterans and low-income persons. Studies by the National Manpower Policy Task Force have shown public employment programs to be a relatively inexpensive and less inflationary way to reduce unemployment.

3. Pre-employment assistance, primarily to: (a) severely disadvantaged adults living in high unemployment areas or persons on welfare, with the aim of improving their prospects of obtaining jobs which can lead to self-support, and (b) low-income youth, in school and out of school, through a combination of part-time or summer jobs and residential or nonresidential training.

4. Efforts to improve the functioning of labor market institutions through overcoming impediments to the flow of workers from labor surplus areas to labor shortage areas, improved labor market information, placement activities, research and development projects, and supportive services to job applicants, all

designed to provide a better match between job seekers and available jobs.

The national scale of these programs in fiscal 1973 was:

	New enrollment (thousands)	Dollars (millions)
Training	390	608
Public employment	112	1,088
Pre-employment assistance		
Adults	175	329
Youth	671	545
Labor market institutions	10,400	646
TOTAL	11,748	3,216

The primary objectives of these manpower programs are: (1) to help disadvantaged persons improve their employability and income and (2) to strengthen the effectiveness of labor market institutions so that the economy can operate more effectively.

Because of the general confusion concerning their objectives, however, all manpower programs cannot be judged by the same set of criteria. Some, like public employment, are designed to reduce unemployment directly by giving jobs to the unemployed. Others are designed mainly to improve the employability of the disadvantaged and not primarily to reduce unemployment directly.

Still others, like all of those measures designed to improve the operation of labor markets, are designed to make the economy work more effectively. At the macroeconomic level, they improve the trade-off between unemployment and inflation by making possible a lower rate of inflation at any given level of unemployment. We shall also see, moreover, that manpower programs can facilitate job creation in rural areas by serving as an attraction for industry.

HUMAN RESOURCE DEVELOPMENT in RURAL TEXAS

Chapter I

RURAL POPULATION AND EMPLOYMENT

Population Changes

Changes in Texas' rural population resemble national trends, with some important differences. In Texas, as in the nation, the agricultural population has declined markedly through time. In the nation, however, the rural nonfarm population has grown large enough to offset the decline in farming, so the total rural population has remained fairly constant at about 54 million since 1910. (The nation's total population has grown since 1910, so the rural population is a declining proportion of the total.) In Texas, by contrast, the rural nonfarm population has not increased enough to offset the farm losses, so total rural population declined from 3,503,435 to 2,261,474 between 1960 and 1970; a majority of Texas' population was rural in 1940 (55 percent), but only about one fifth of the state's population remained in rural areas in 1970. In 1920, almost half (48 percent) of the state's *rural* population lived on farms, but by 1970 this proportion declined to about one fifth (20.5 percent).

These general changes in the state's population conceal considerable variation in different parts of the state. For analytical purposes, we have divided the state into the four regions depicted in Figure 1. The analysis reveals three distinct nonmetropolitan regions and a fourth grouping that includes all metropolitan areas of the state. The eastern nonmetropolitan region has a minority population of approximately 25 percent, a large proportion of which is black. Within the eastern portion of the state also is a large metropolitan population (included in Region IV), which makes industrial development in rural areas more a metropolitan

Figure 1

POPULATION REGIONS OF TEXAS

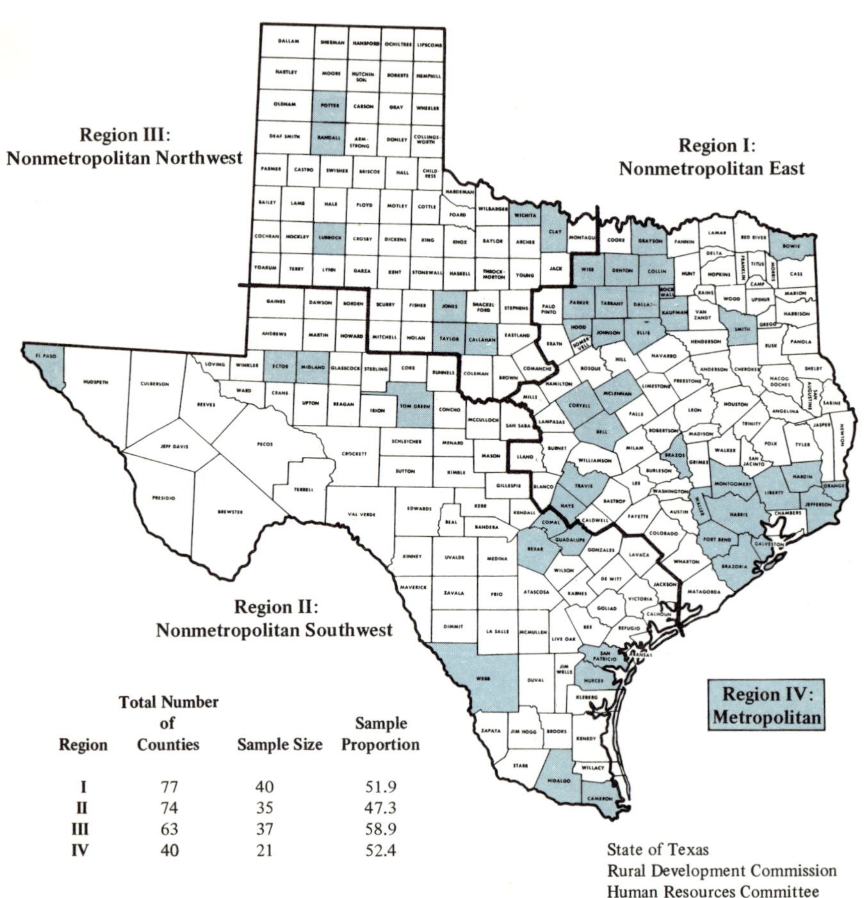

Region	Total Number of Counties	Sample Size	Sample Proportion
I	77	40	51.9
II	74	35	47.3
III	63	37	58.9
IV	40	21	52.4

State of Texas
Rural Development Commission
Human Resources Committee

"spin-off" phenomenon than elsewhere. The southwest nonmetropolitan region was designed to hold the entire border together as a statistical unit, since most of the industry and Mexican American population of southwestern Texas is concentrated on the border. The northwest nonmetropolitan region is a predominantly agricultural area with a relatively small minority population; no major metropolitan area lies within its boundaries. The fourth region is metropolitan Texas as defined in 1970.

Table 1 shows the populations of these regions in 1960 and 1970; the metropolitan counties in the east grew by 32.4 percent as compared with 8.1 percent for nonmetropolitan areas. The main nonmetropolitan losses were heaviest in the northwestern counties,

Table 1

TEXAS POPULATION AND POPULATION CHANGES BY REGION, 1960-1970

Region	1970 Population	1960 Population	Percent change in population
East	7,145,902	5,671,256	26.0
Metropolitan	5,538,003	4,184,275	32.4
Nonmetropolitan	1,607,899	1,486,981	8.1
Southwest	2,911,964	2,716,217	7.2
Metropolitan	2,083,896	1,872,270	11.3
Nonmetropolitan	828,068	843,947	– 1.9
Northwest	1,138,594	1,213,220	– 6.1
Metropolitan	565,271	555,783	1.7
Nonmetropolitan	573,323	657,437	– 12.8
Total metropolitan	8,187,170	6,612,328	23.8
Total nonmetropolitan	3,009,290	2,988,365	.7
State	11,196,400	9,600,693	16.6

Source: Bureau of the Census, U.S. Department of Commerce, *General Social and Economic Characteristics of Texas*, PC(1)-C45.

where a decline of 12.8 percent caused a total population decline of 6.1 percent. The slight nonmetropolitan decline in the southwestern counties (1.9 percent) was more than offset by the 11.3-percent growth in metropolitan counties, causing a population growth of 7.2 percent. In the state as a whole, the metropolitan population grew by 23.8 percent and the nonmetropolitan by .7 percent, resulting in an overall gain of 16.6 percent.

There is considerable variation in the racial and ethnic composition of the three regions of Texas (see Table 2). The black population is concentrated mainly in the east, while Mexican Americans are heavily concentrated in the two western regions.

Trends, Dimensions, Locations, and Characteristics of the Rural Labor Force in Texas

Relative to metropolitan areas, the labor force in nonmetropolitan Texas is older, poorer, and less educated, has less gainful employment, and supports a larger dependent population. The

Table 2

DISTRIBUTION OF MINORITY POPULATION BY REGION IN TEXAS, 1970
(Metropolitan included in respective regions)

Region	Proportion black in 1970	Proportion Spanish-surnamed in 1970*
East	17.0	7.5
Southwest	8.1	25.5
Northwest	5.3	16.7
Total Texas	12.7	16.9

* Estimated by Spanish-surnamed school enrollment from Texas Office of Economic Opportunity, *Poverty in Texas* (1972).

Source: Texas Office of Economic Opportunity, *Poverty in Texas* (1972).

average age in nonmetropolitan areas is 30 years, in metropolitan areas, 25.5 years. The average belies to some extent the nature of the relative age distributions. Whereas the proportion of children 14 and younger in metropolitan and nonmetropolitan areas is approximately the same, over 13 percent of the nonmetropolitan and about 7 percent of the metropolitan population are 65 years of age or more. The difference is made up in the prime working ages, 25 to 44, where over one fourth of the metropolitan population and only one fifth of the nonmetropolitan population are concentrated. As Table 3 shows, the proportion of Texans 25-44 years of age was 26 percent in metropolitan and only 19.8 percent in nonmetropolitan areas. A relatively smaller number, therefore, of prime working-age adults live in rural areas.

The difference in the size of the prime working-age population is a major factor accounting for the higher incidence of poverty, the lower educational attainment levels, and the lower labor force participation rates in rural areas as compared with metropolitan areas.

The ratios in Table 4 provide a clearer picture of the extent of dependency in various Texas regions. The dependency ratio in nonmetropolitan Texas was 66.8 percent, as compared with 60.9 percent for metropolitan areas.

Table 3

PROPORTION OF POPULATION OF PRIME WORKING AGE (25-44) IN TEXAS

Region	Proportion of population of prime working age (25-44)
East nonmetropolitan	18.7
Southwest nonmetropolitan	21.5
Northwest nonmetropolitan	21.2
Metropolitan	26.0
Nonmetropolitan total	19.8

Source: See statistical appendix.

Table 4

DEPENDENCY RATIOS FOR REGIONS IN TEXAS, 1970*

Region	Proportion of population ages 0-14 years	Proportion of population ages 65 and over	Dependency ratio
East	25.6	14.3	66.4
Southwest	30.7	11.4	72.7
Northwest	27.6	13.6	70.0
Metropolitan	30.8	7.3	60.9
Total nonmetropolitan	26.9	13.1	66.8

* Adapted from Texas Office of Economic Opportunity, *Poverty in Texas* (1972). The dependency ratio is the number of persons ages 0-14 plus the number of persons ages 65 and over divided by the number of persons ages 15-64 multiplied by 100. This table represents a complete count of Texas counties.

Table 5

PROPORTION OF POVERTY FAMILIES IN METROPOLITAN AND NONMETROPOLITAN TEXAS, 1960 AND 1970

Region	Proportion of families receiving less than $3,000 in 1960	Proportion of families receiving less than $4,000 in 1970	Ratio of 1970 to 1960 proportions
East nonmetropolitan	39.8	28.1	70.6
Southwest nonmetropolitan	38.0	28.5	75.0
Northwest nonmetropolitan	32.3	24.9	77.1
Metropolitan	23.4	15.7	67.1
Nonmetropolitan total	37.9	27.5	72.6

Source: See statistical appendix.

The incidence of poverty is greater in nonmetropolitan areas than in metropolitan, and nonmetropolitan areas shared unequally in the reductions in the incidence of poverty throughout the 1960s (see Table 5).

Even for those holding permanent jobs, the incidence of poverty is 15 percent in nonmetropolitan areas, compared with 10.8 percent in metropolitan areas. In 1970, 27.5 percent of Texas nonmetropolitan families received less than $4,000, as compared with only 15.7 percent for metropolitan areas. Use of $3,000 as the poverty cut-off level in 1960 results in comparable figures of 23.4 percent for metropolitan areas and 37.9 percent for nonmetropolitan areas. By 1970 the metropolitan poverty population had declined to 67.1 percent of the 1960 poverty population, while the corresponding figure for nonmetropolitan areas was 72.6 percent. Moreover, the 1970 incidence of nonmetropolitan poverty was higher (27.5 percent) than it had been in metropolitan areas ten years earlier (23.4 percent).

The difference in the incidence of poverty between Texas' three major ethnic groups—blacks, Chicanos, and Anglos—was one of the major findings of the Texas Household Survey conducted by the Texas Office of Economic Opportunity.[1] The findings revealed the following poverty rates: blacks, 44 percent; Chicanos, 45.3 percent; and Anglos, 12.6 percent. Although blacks and Chicanos together constituted less than one third (29.4 percent) of the total Texas population, they accounted for nearly 60 percent of the poor population. The minorities also carried more than their share of poverty-related behavior patterns. For example, black males were less likely to be in the labor force and more likely to remain as nonworkers through time. Chicanos were less likely to have been enrolled in school during the years they should have been finishing high school (see regression analysis, Table A-4, statistical appendix).

These results, all consistent with the general picture of the inferior socioeconomic status of minorities in nonmetropolitan Texas, suggest that minorities have special needs for human resource development programs aimed at preparing them for the

[1]Texas Office of Economic Opportunity, *Poverty in Texas* (Austin, Texas: Department of Community Affairs, State of Texas, 1972).

labor market. They also suggest that there is further need to assure that as minorities improve their levels of education and training, they are not frustrated by discriminatory employment patterns. Detailed analysis of black employment problems in nonmetropolitan areas of other Southern states reveals clearly that blacks continue to face discriminatory employment patterns that block their upward occupational mobility and lead to their outmigration to metropolitan ghettos.[2] The problem is similar in nonmetropolitan Texas, where there exists a significant gap between blacks and whites in terms of employment growth rates and average occupational levels. Despite considerable progress in terms of employment opportunities for minorities, nonmetropolitan Texas, like metropolitan areas throughout Texas and the nation, clearly has a need for antidiscrimination programs that break down the patterns of institutionalized discrimination.

Composition of Rural Farm and Nonfarm Employment

Until revised data become available and a detailed analysis can be undertaken, this analysis of rural farm and nonfarm populations must be incomplete,[3] but something can be learned from the information available. For example, rural poverty is becoming more and more a nonfarm phenomenon, as over five sixths of the total population in rural areas is nonfarm. Many of these nonfarm residents cannot find employment opportunities in the area and are at the same time highly immobile. For example, nearly 20 percent of the rural nonfarm residents have lived in the same house for over twenty years, whereas the comparable figure for metropolitan areas is approximately 10 percent. On the other hand, there is a mobile element of the rural nonfarm population, a large segment of which relates to job aspirations. The intercounty movement of individuals, for reasons other than service in the armed forces and college attendance, between 1965 and 1970 is greater for Texans

[2] James L. Walker, "Economic Development, Black Employment, and Black Migration in the Nonmetropolitan Deep South," Ph.D. dissertation, The University of Texas at Austin, 1973.

[3] The revision of rural farm and rural nonfarm data is being published now and is particularly vital in answering this question thoroughly.

in the rural nonfarm group than for those living in metropolitan areas.

The rural nonfarm population is expected to increase throughout the 1970s. This particularly strategic group comprises relatively highly mobile and immobile segments. The source of growth in this population, the job aspirations, the levels of education and skill, and the age and dependency characteristics are all critical variables in the formulation of a rural manpower policy.

Although limited data are available on labor mobility, Table 6 does indicate a strategic difference in the experience of males 30-49 years old (in 1970) in labor market experience, by region, in Texas. These figures indicate that nonmetropolitan males in this prime working-age group in 1965 were much less likely to be working in 1970 (9.1 percent contrasted with 13.9 percent for their metropolitan counterparts), and a significantly higher proportion had become nonworkers by 1970 (20.9 percent for nonmetropolitan areas, 9.4 percent for metropolitan areas). The nonworking rates were particularly high in the east (21.6 percent), and the decline in nonworker status was especially low in the northwest.

Table 6

LABOR MOBILITY FOR MALES, 30-49 YEARS OF AGE, FOR METROPOLITAN AND NONMETROPOLITAN TEXAS, 1970

Region	Nonworker, 1965; worker, 1970 (1)	Nonworker, 1965; nonworker, 1970 (2)	Worker, 1965; nonworker, 1970 (3)	Total, columns (2) and (3)
East	9.3	14.0	7.6	21.6
Southwest	9.4	12.8	4.3	17.1
Northwest	4.2	6.6	7.2	13.8
Metropolitan	13.9	6.0	5.4	9.4
Total nonmetropolitan	9.1	13.6	7.3	20.9

Source: See statistical appendix.

Although the rural farm and nonfarm data needed to test displacement directly are not available, the movement probably is largely a movement from farm work to nonfarm nonwork at a rate of 7 percent. For those in nonmetropolitan areas of prime working age not working in 1965, the picture is hardly bright: Over 13 percent were not working in 1970.

Education

Although the 1970 median educational level in nonmetropolitan areas was low (10.3 years) relative to metropolitan areas (12.1 years), the educational level of young people was greater than that of their forebears, yet still significantly below that of their metropolitan counterparts. Those individuals in rural (as opposed to nonmetropolitan) areas 18 to 24 years old in 1970 completed high school at a rate of less than 50 percent, compared to over 60 percent in urban areas. Not surprisingly, then, the incidence of poverty for the 15-24 age group in SMSAs was below the incidence for the 0-14 age group, whereas in nonmetropolitan areas the incidence increased from 27.3 percent in the 0-14 age group to 28.4 percent in the 15-24 age group.

The obvious importance of education to "successful" labor market performance necessitates a closer look at regional variations. As Table 7 indicates, in 1970 the proportion of persons over 25 who entered high school is lower in nonmetropolitan areas (61.1 percent for males, as compared with 71 percent for metropolitan areas; for females, 66.5 percent, as compared with 72.3 percent for metropolitan areas). Moreover, among those who did enter high schools, the dropout rate (proportion having some high school but no diploma) was higher in nonmetropolitan areas (36.2 percent for males, 40.2 percent for females) than in metropolitan areas (27.4 percent and 31.7 percent).

Even though the official unemployment rates differ little between metropolitan and nonmetropolitan markets, the labor force participation of both males and females is much lower in nonmetropolitan areas. The relatively low participation rates in rural areas are apparently strongly related to the age distribution, although probably a different constellation of factors determines

Table 7

SECONDARY-EDUCATION BACKGROUND OF TEXANS OVER 25, BY REGION AND SEX, 1960 AND 1970 (percent)

	Males				Females			
	Attended high school		Attended high school, no diploma		Attended high school		Attended high school, no diploma	
Region	1960	1970	1960	1970	1960	1970	1960	1970
East	48.1	61.6	39.1	36.5	55.3	67.3	21.9	27.9
Southwest	46.3	55.5	36.5	33.6	50.9	59.2	35.6	37.2
Northwest	57.7	65.3	40.0	37.7	65.0	71.6	39.5	39.5
Metropolitan	60.1	71.0	30.1	27.4	63.1	72.3	31.6	31.7
Nonmetropolitan total	50.1	61.1	38.8	36.2	56.8	66.5	38.8	40.2

Source: See statistical appendix.

Table 8

FEMALE HEADS OF POVERTY FAMILIES BY REGION IN TEXAS, 1970

Region	Proportion of females heading poverty families, 1970
East	22.0
Southwest	19.2
Northwest	16.5
Metropolitan	34.8
Total nonmetropolitan	21.7

Source: See statistical appendix.

participation in rural areas as opposed to urban. One indication of a difference is the proportion of poor families headed by females (see Table 8). In the metropolitan areas of Texas, approximately one third (34.8 percent) of poor families are headed by females (compared with one half nationwide), whereas in nonmetropolitan Texas about one fifth (21.7 percent) of poor families have female heads (compared with one fourth for the nation). Moreover, in female-headed poor households there were variations between Texas nonmetropolitan regions, ranging from 22 percent in East Texas to 16.5 percent in the northwestern part of the state.

In Texas relatively fewer female-headed poverty families live in nonmetropolitan areas than in metropolitan ones. Moreover, as compared with the nation, where about half of the poor families are headed by males, nonmetropolitan poverty is much more of a male phenomenon—well over three fourths of all poor families (78.3 percent) being headed by males. This fact, in combination with the rapid displacement of males from rural jobs, suggests a need for special programs to provide income for men in nonmetropolitan Texas.

Major Factors Influencing Rural Labor Force Participation Rates

The labor force participation rates in nonmetropolitan areas of Texas exhibit patterns somewhat unlike those in metropolitan areas. Table 9 lists the percent in the labor force by age and sex for metropolitan areas and for nonmetropolitan categories.

The labor force participation rates of prime-working-age individuals in the urban areas of nonmetropolitan Texas are quite similar to those of metropolitan Texas. There are relatively fewer prime-working-age males in nonmetropolitan areas, however, especially in East Texas. Among the prime-working-age males, only in the rural nonfarm sector is labor participation significantly below metropolitan rates (the rural nonfarm data are not conclusive owing to census sampling error and are in the process of being adjusted). The female participation rates in both rural farm and rural nonfarm sectors are somewhat below metropolitan rates.

The prime-working-age pattern of labor force participation, relative to that of metropolitan areas, is replicated in most, but not all, age groups. Higher participation rates for rural farm males ages 20 to 24 represent an obvious break in the pattern. Rural youth and rural nonfarm individuals participate to a smaller degree than

Table 9

PERCENT IN LABOR FORCE BY AGE AND SEX IN METROPOLITAN AND NONMETROPOLITAN AREAS OF TEXAS, 1970

Age and sex	Metropolitan	Nonmetropolitan			
		Total	Urban	Rural nonfarm	Rural farm
Male					
16 and 17	34.8	30.6	36.4	25.0	28.1
18 and 19	61.6	55.5	58.2	52.1	51.8
20 and 21	76.5	79.4	81.2	74.6	77.3
22 to 24	87.2	87.8	88.0	87.3	88.1
25 to 34	94.6	92.8	93.2	91.6	95.2
35 to 44	95.6	93.2	93.2	92.4	95.3
45 to 64	88.8	84.1	85.5	81.0	87.3
65 and over	29.8	29.2	28.1	23.7	47.3
Female					
16 and 17	19.1	15.8	19.3	12.9	10.9
18 and 19	44.3	32.7	33.7	31.1	31.6
20 and 21	54.7	42.5	43.9	39.4	42.4
22 to 24	56.7	42.5	45.1	39.4	34.5
25 to 34	47.5	40.9	44.9	37.3	32.9
35 to 44	51.1	48.2	52.3	46.1	37.2
45 to 64	47.5	42.0	48.2	38.9	30.2
65 and over	11.7	9.4	10.8	7.9	7.8

Source: See statistical appendix.

metropolitan residents of the same age. This factor, along with the nonmetropolitan age distribution, explains to a large degree the overall low participation rates in nonmetropolitan areas and undoubtedly is due in large measure to the relative scarcity of job opportunities in rural areas.

It is commonly assumed that labor force participation rates are influenced by the availability of welfare payments as an alternative to work. Although the available data do not provide an answer to this question, they do make it possible to conclude that welfare payments cannot be responsible for the lower participation rates in rural areas, because the proportion of families receiving welfare or public assistance relative to those in poverty is about the same in metropolitan and nonmetropolitan areas, although the nonmetropolitan welfare recipient rates and incidences of poverty are higher (see Table 10). However, the overall ratio of nonmetropolitan welfare recipients to poor people is due to the relatively low ratio in East Texas (2.54); in the other regions, the ratios (3.58 and 3.73) are much higher than for the metropolitan counties (2.86).

The more obvious policy alternatives for the state include expansion of programs such as the Neighborhood Youth Corps and Operation Mainstream. Controls on local implementation must be exercised in combination with program development so that the purposes of such programs are not undermined. While the incidence of poverty in nonmetropolitan areas is 28.4 percent among the 15-24 age group, rural areas received only 16.6 percent of Neighborhood Youth Corps (out-of-school) funds in fiscal 1973.

Table 10

PROPORTION OF TEXAS FAMILIES IN POVERTY AND RECEIVING WELFARE, BY REGION, 1970

Region	Families in poverty (1)	Percent of families in poverty (2)	Percent of families receiving welfare (3)	(2)/(3)
East	80,157	19.3	7.6	2.54
Southwest	46,963	22.6	6.3	3.58
Northwest	26,018	16.8	4.5	3.73
Total metropolitan	254,561	12.6	4.4	2.86
Total nonmetropolitan	151,919	19.5	6.6	2.80

Source: See statistical appendix.

Subemployment

It has long been recognized that the rate of unemployment is an inadequate measure of the looseness or tightness of labor markets, because it does not count those who are not working or who are working part time, at low wages, or below their capacities; unemployment is a measure of those who are willing and able to work and are actively seeking jobs. We lack adequate measures of those who are working part time and below their capacities, but it is possible to obtain a "subemployment rate" by adjusting the unemployment rate for working-age people who are not working and working poor heads of households for 1970. For 1960,

Table 11

SUBEMPLOYMENT BY SEX IN THE NONMETROPOLITAN EAST, 1960-1970

Estimates	Males 1960	Females 1960	Males 1970	Females 1970
Population over 14*	510,127	504,978	580,665	584,417
Civilian labor force	317,276	139,736	350,518	205,473
Participation rate	62.2	27.7	60.4	35.2
Unemployment	25,670	23,177	35,467	12,355
Unemployment rate	8.1	16.6	10.1	6.0
Proportion of nonparticipants** under 65 who are employable	29,054	24,277	21,420	22,334
Adjusted unemployment rate	15.8	28.9	15.3	15.2
Working poor family heads†	n.a.	n.a.	36,413	6,228
Nonmetropolitan subemployment rate	n.a.	n.a.	25.1	17.8

* Changes to population over 16 years of age in 1970.

** For males, the proportion used is 50 percent of nonparticipants; for females, the proportion is 10 percent. The calculated value is added both to the civilian labor force and to the unemployment to calculate the adjusted unemployment rate.

† The number of working poor family heads is added to unemployment and adjusted unemployment to calculate rate of subemployment.

Source: See statistical appendix.

adjustments can be made for working-age people who are not working, but data on working poor heads of families are not available for that year.

Tables 11 through 15 contain the results of these calculations. Because of lower nonmetropolitan labor force participation rates, adjustments for nonworkers raise the unemployment rate for nonmetropolitan males from 5.9 percent to 12 percent in 1960 and from 3 percent to 7.9 percent in 1970; the comparable figures for metropolitan areas are 5.4 percent to 8.1 percent for 1970 and 3 percent to 6.2 percent for 1970. Thus, although the metropolitan and nonmetropolitan unemployment rates for males were identical in 1970, the adjusted unemployment rate is much higher for nonmetropolitan areas, and the subemployment rate climbs even higher—11.8 percent for metropolitan areas and 18.5 percent for nonmetropolitan areas. For males, the subemployment rate is 3.27 times the unemployment rate for metropolitan areas and 6.27 times that of the nonmetropolitan (see Table 16). For nonmetropolitan females, the unemployment rate was 5.7 percent in 1970

Table 12

SUBEMPLOYMENT BY SEX IN THE NONMETROPOLITAN SOUTHWEST, 1960-1970*

Estimates	Males 1960	Females 1960	Males 1970	Females 1970
Population over 14	295,139	300,489	267,373	286,713
Civilian labor force	220,178	81,818	192,230	98,616
Participation rate	74.6	27.2	71.9	34.4
Unemployment	10,104	5,315	8,127	5,036
Unemployment rate	4.6	6.5	4.2	5.1
Proportion of nonparticipants under 65 who are employable	8,230	14,713	9,098	12,450
Adjusted unemployment rate	8.0	20.7	8.6	15.7
Working poor family heads	n.a.	n.a.	28,413	3,204
Nonmetropolitan subemployment rate	n.a.	n.a.	22.7	18.6

* Notes from Table 11 apply to this table.

Source: See statistical appendix.

Table 13

SUBEMPLOYMENT BY SEX IN THE NONMETROPOLITAN NORTHWEST, 1960-1970*

Estimates	Males 1960	Females 1960	Males 1970	Females 1970
Population over 14	220,643	222,027	192,470	211,741
Civilian labor force	171,258	60,500	146,515	71,949
Participation rate	77.6	27.2	76.1	34.0
Unemployment	5,610	6,766	4,018	4,024
Unemployment rate	3.3	11.2	2.7	5.6
Proportion of nonparticipants under 65 who are employable	10,892	11,384	5,768	8,684
Adjusted unemployment rate	9.1	25.2	6.9	15.8
Working poor family heads	n.a.	n.a.	11,819	1,331
Nonmetropolitan subemployment rate	n.a.	n.a.	15.2	17.4

* Notes from Table 11 apply to this table.
Source: See statistical appendix.

and the subemployment rate was 18 percent, or 3.16 times as large; the comparable metropolitan rates were 4.4 percent and 15 percent, or 3.41 times as great. Thus, relative to metropolitan areas, the unemployment rate greatly underestimates the subemployment of nonmetropolitan males, but not females. (This conclusion is compatible with the general finding of deteriorating employment opportunities for rural males and the fact that Texas has a much larger proportion of male-headed poverty families than the nation as a whole.) For males and females, unemployment underestimates subemployment in nonmetropolitan areas. Therefore, any use of unemployment as an allocation of funds, as was done for the Emergency Employment Act of 1971, is biased against nonmetropolitan areas in terms of subemployment, a more accurate measure of need than unemployment.

Tables 11 through 13 reveal considerable variation among regions in the ratio of unemployment to subemployment for males. In East Texas, unemployment was 10.1 percent and subemployment 25.1 percent; in Southwest Texas, unemployment was 4.2

percent and subemployment 22.7 percent; and in Northwest Texas, unemployment was 2.7 percent and subemployment 15.2 percent. Thus the male subemployment rate is 2.5 times as great as the unemployment rate in East Texas, where the unemployment rate is highest, 5.4 times as great in Southwest Texas, and 5.63 times as great in the northwest.

Changes in Rural Employment by Major Groups

While the state experienced a healthy 24.8-percent rate of growth in total employment between 1960 and 1970, the nonmetropolitan areas were confined to a much slower 2.9-percent growth rate and a net gain of only 29,000 jobs. The major restraining factor was the decline by almost 76,000 jobs in the agricultural, forestry, and fishery industries (see Table 17). In addition, major declines occurred in the mining and private

Table 14

SUBEMPLOYMENT BY SEX IN METROPOLITAN AREAS, 1960-1970*

Estimates	Males 1960	Females 1960	Males 1970	Females 1970
Population over 14	1,961,503	2,229,810	2,607,709	2,846,666
Civilian labor force	1,592,014	796,688	1,993,359	1,228,289
Participation rate	81.2	35.7	76.4	43.1
Unemployment	86,036	36,319	59,720	53,942
Unemployment rate	5.4	4.6	3.0	4.4
Proportion of nonparticipants under 65 who are employable	46,362	100,214	68,377	111,258
Adjusted unemployment rate	8.1	15.2	6.2	12.3
Working poor family heads	n.a.	n.a.	115,409	36,186
Nonmetropolitan subemployment rate	n.a.	n.a.	11.8	15.0

* Notes from Table 11 apply to this table.
Source: See statistical appendix.

Table 15

SUBEMPLOYMENT BY SEX IN NONMETROPOLITAN AREAS, 1960-1970*

Estimates	Males 1960	Females 1960	Males 1970	Females 1970
Population over 14	1,024,153	1,024,498	1,046,089	1,086,824
Civilian labor force	703,832	281,391	689,603	377,571
Participation rate	68.7	27.5	65.9	34.7
Unemployment	41,682	36,425	20,922	21,652
Unemployment rate	5.9	12.9	3.0	5.7
Proportion of nonparticipants under 65 who are employable	49,030	50,247	36,423	43,392
Adjusted unemployment rate	12.0	26.1	7.9	15.5
Working poor family heads	n.a.	n.a.	76,645	10,646
Nonmetropolitan subemployment rate	n.a.	n.a.	18.5	18.0

* Notes from Table 11 apply to this table. The values in this table differ from the total of individual nonmetropolitan regions owing to sampling error in the individual regions.

Source: See statistical appendix.

Table 16

UNEMPLOYMENT AND SUBEMPLOYMENT FOR MALES, BY REGION, 1960 AND 1970

Region	Unemployment (percent) 1960	Unemployment (percent) 1970	Subemployment (percent) 1970	Subemployment / Unemployment 1970
East	8.1	10.1	25.1	2.48
Southwest	4.6	4.2	22.7	5.40
Northwest	3.3	2.7	15.2	5.63
Total nonmetropolitan	5.9	3.0	18.8	6.27
Total metropolitan	5.4	3.0	11.8	3.93

Source: See statistical appendix.

Table 17

CHANGES IN EMPLOYMENT BY INDUSTRY IN NONMETROPOLITAN TEXAS, 1960-1970

Industry	1960	1970	Change in employment	Percent change in employment	Percent change in total Texas employment
Total employment	981,373	1,009,594	29,221	2.9	24.8
Agriculture, forestry, and fisheries	198,629	122,763	– 75,866	– 38.2	– 36.0
Mining	51,202	39,594	– 11,608	– 22.7	– 1.3
Construction	79,111	81,142	2,031	2.6	21.5
Manufacturing	118,445	141,634	23,189	22.1	35.9
Durable goods	54,656	78,091	23,435	42.8	68.9
Nondurable goods	63,789	63,543	– 246	– 0.4	11.3
Railroads	13,516	9,464	– 4,052	– 30.0	– 32.1
Trucking and warehousing	13,972	12,721	– 1,251	– 9.0	12.2
Other transportation	9,702	8,804	– 898	– 9.3	19.5
Communications	9,437	10,708	1,271	13.5	26.3
Utilities and sanitary services	18,112	21,309	3,197	17.7	27.1
Wholesale trade	26,630	28,319	1,689	6.3	34.6
Food, bakery, and dairy stores	31,201	28,348	2,853	– 9.1	5.9
Eating and drinking	31,966	32,089	123	0.4	18.3
Other retail trade	109,505	120,866	11,361	10.4	46.2
Finance, insurance, and real estate	23,826	30,857	7,031	29.5	48.1
Business service and repair	22,017	23,559	1,542	7.0	55.3
Private household service	44,407	28,298	– 16,109	– 36.3	– 39.0
Other personal service	35,293	38,267	2,974	8.4	20.8
Entertainment and recreation	54,644	6,013	549	10.0	24.0
Hospital and health services	21,615	51,957	30,342	140.4	172.9

Industry	1960	1970	Change in employment	Percent change in employment	Percent change in total Texas employment
Education	57,161	85,119	27,958	48.9	238.9
Welfare, religion, and nonprofit	11,861	12,900	1,039	8.8	26.6
Legal, engineering, and other	13,962	16,948	2,986	21.4	32.6
Public administration	38,542	47,139	8,597	22.3	33.0

Source: See statistical appendix.

household services sectors, with losses of 11,600 and 16,100 jobs respectively. The employment situation also deteriorated somewhat in nondurable goods manufacturing and in the transportation sectors. While the remaining industrial sectors were all expanding in nonmetropolitan areas, they all were growing at a lower percentage rate than was the case for the state as a whole. For example, while nonmetropolitan construction was growing at a rate of 2.6 percent, the growth rate for construction statewide was 21.5 percent, and while durable goods manufacturing grew at a rate of 42.8 percent in nonmetropolitan areas, the rate statewide was 68.9 percent.

In general, the nonmetropolitan growth rate was much slower than that of metropolitan areas, primarily because of the overconcentration of agriculture in nonmetropolitan areas. The massive declines in agricultural employment meant a diminishing economic base for many areas, hence sectors that depended on local spending were also forced to cut back. Manufacturing grew at a 22.1-percent rate between 1960 and 1970, but the 23,200 jobs gained were not enough to offset the massive losses in agriculture. While other economic base activities, such as hospitals and health services, education, and public administration, were all expanding, the combined increase of all economic base activities was barely sufficient to overcome the agricultural losses and to generate the slow overall growth rate.

Whether the growth rates of the nonagricultural economic base activities will continue in the 1970s depends upon many variables, but if they can be maintained or accelerated, the impact on derivative employment sectors, and on overall employment, will be much greater.

The employment picture in nonmetropolitan Texas varies considerably between regions (see statistical appendix, Tables A-1, A-2, and A-3). Employment in the nonmetropolitan east grew at a 13.5-percent rate overall. While this was not sufficient to offset the 26-percent growth in population, it clearly was better than the absolute total employment declines of 4.1 percent in the nonmetropolitan southwest and 9.4 percent in the nonmetropolitan northwest. There are three basic reasons for the differences. First, the eastern region was less concentrated in agricultural employment than the other two regions. Conversely, it was much more heavily concentrated in manufacturing employment. Third, the manufacturing growth rate was higher in the eastern region. These

Table 18

NUMBER OF FARMS IN TEXAS AND THE UNITED STATES, BY DECADE, 1900-1970

	Texas		United States	
Year	Number of farms	Percentage change from preceding decade	Number of farms	Percentage change from preceding decade
1900	352,190		5,738,000	
1910	418,000	18.7	6,362,000	10.9
1920	446,000	6.7	6,518,000	2.5
1930	496,000	11.2	6,546,000	0.4
1940	420,000	− 15.3	6,350,000	− 3.0
1950	345,000	− 17.9	5,648,000	− 11.1
1960	246,000	− 28.7	3,962,000	− 29.9
1970	188,000	− 23.6	2,924,000	− 26.2

Source: U.S. Department of Agriculture, Statistical Reporting Service, *Number of Farms—1910-1959, Land in Farms—1950-1959, by States*, June 1962; U.S. Department of Agriculture, *Yearbook of the United States—1901*, 1902, p. 785; U.S. Bureau of the Census, *Statistical Abstract of the United States*, 94th ed., 1973, p. 586; U.S. Bureau of the Census, *Historical Statistics of the United States, 1789-1945*, 1949, p. 96.

Table 19

AVERAGE SIZE OF FARMS IN TEXAS AND THE UNITED STATES, BY DECADE, 1900-1970

	Texas		United States	
Year	Acres per farm	Percentage change from preceding decade	Acres per farm	Percentage change from preceding decade
1900	357	– 24.6	146	– 5.5
1910	269		138	
1920	256	– 4.8	147	6.5
1930	251	– 2.0	151	2.7
1940	328	30.7	167	10.6
1950	421	28.4	213	27.5
1960	626	48.7	297	39.4
1970	771	23.2	383	29.0

Source: U.S. Bureau of the Census, *Statistical Abstract of the United States*, 43rd, 63rd, 74th, and 94th eds.; U.S. Bureau of the Census, *Historical Statistics of the United States, 1789-1945*, 1949, p. 96.

differences suggest that policies for nonmetropolitan Texas will have to be differentiated by region.

The projections in the statistical appendix reveal that the prospects for further growth also differ between the regions.

Composition and Future of Texas Agricultural Employment

In Texas, as in the nation, there has been a long-term trend toward fewer but larger farms. Moreover, the trend toward greater size appears to be more evident for Texas than for the nation as a whole. From 1930 to 1970, the number of Texas farms decreased 62 percent, with average farm size increasing by 207 percent. During the same period, for the United States, the number of farms decreased by 55 percent, with average farm size increasing by 154 percent.

For Texas and the nation, there has been a trend toward increased concentration in agricultural production. In terms of the cash receipts from farm production, 50 percent of Texas farms produced 94.2 percent of agricultural sales in 1959 and 95.8 percent in 1969.[4] For the United States, 50 percent of farms produced 92.7 percent of sales in 1960 and 95.4 percent in 1972.[5]

In 1970 Texas led the nation in the production of cattle, sheep and wool, goats and mohair, and cotton. Because of different labor requirements, however, these crops do not account for the same proportions of the state's $3,053,536,000 cash receipts for 1969 or for wages paid to agricultural employment. The proportions were as follows:

Crops	Gross receipts (percent)	Wages (percent)
Livestock	45.3%	29.7%
Cash grain and other field crops	21.1%	26.8%
Cotton	11.9%	19.3%
Other	21.7%	24.2%

Source: *Texas Food and Fiber Facts, 1972*, Texas A&M University, Texas Agricultural Extension Services and Texas Experiment Station, 1972.

Most of the Texas agricultural work force is composed of either unpaid family workers or hired farm labor from local areas—that is, they do not have to leave home overnight to do temporary work. In 1969, for example, local labor accounted for over 99 percent of Texas seasonal agricultural employment in January, February, and March and well over 90 percent for all other months except July and August, when the proportions were 83.7 percent and 87 percent, respectively. Moreover, almost all of the nonlocal agricultural labor came from within the state.[6]

As the number of farms in Texas declines and the size of those remaining increases, the number of year-round farm jobs has increased for all areas except the Lower Rio Grande Valley, where

[4]U.S. Bureau of the Census, *United States Census of Agriculture—1959*, vol. 1, part 37, pp. 36, 37, 42, and 43; U.S. Bureau of the Census, *United States Census of Agriculture—1969*, sec. I, part 37, pp. 3, 7, and 108.

[5]U.S. Department of Agriculture, Economic Research Service, *Farm Income Situation*, FIS-222, July 1973, pp. 68-71.

[6]Texas Employment Commission, *Texas Farm Labor Annual Report, 1970* (Austin, Texas: Texas Employment Commission, 1970), p. 7.

the number of such jobs declined by 2.9 percent between 1962 and 1969, as compared with an *increase* of regular year-round farm jobs of 37 percent in the rest of the state for the same period. Moreover, according to the Texas Employment Commission the number of seasonal farm jobs declined faster in the Lower Rio Grande Valley—by 63 percent, compared with a total of 58.5 percent for the state. The Texas Employment Commission drew this conclusion with respect to the Lower Rio Grande Valley:

> Needless to say, the employability problems brought on by poor education, language barriers and cultural deprivation which burden the seasonal farm worker are intensified by the weak economic environment in which most of them reside.[7]

Declining agricultural employment in Texas has primarily affected nonmetropolitan males. While the state as a whole lost roughly 110,000 jobs in agriculture, forestry, and fisheries between 1960 and 1970, the nonmetropolitan areas sustained a loss of almost 76,000 jobs. Nonmetropolitan agricultural losses were heavily concentrated among males. Male farmers and farm managers lost some 51,600 jobs, while females lost only about 2,100 such positions. In the farm laborer category, males lost over 17,100 jobs and females lost only 4,200 jobs.

Agricultural employment declined more rapidly in the eastern nonmetropolitan region, where the loss was almost 47 percent, as compared with declines of 38 percent in the southwest and 27 percent in the northwest. This probably is related to the fact that the eastern region is heavily black, and blacks lost employment in agriculture at a much greater rate than whites. This can be seen from the figures for all of nonmetropolitan Texas. While all male farmers and farm managers declined at a rate of 47 percent between 1960 and 1970, black males left the same occupations at rates of 82 percent. The picture is similar for the category of male farm laborers, where blacks lost 43 percent and total males lost only 27 percent during this period.

Another way to consider this unremitting attrition of agricultural employment opportunities is to examine seasonal farm

---

[7] *Ibid.*, p. 9.

placements by the Texas Employment Commission. In 1967 a total of 263,000 seasonal farm placements were made. By 1970 the total number of placements had declined by over 25 percent, to a total of only 195,000.[8]

The composition of Texas agriculture has been changing toward larger farms; increased emphasis has been placed on the production of livestock, poultry, and their products and increased mechanization. While the number of farms in the 1-49 acre class declined by 1 percent between 1964 and 1969, the number of farms in the 50-499 acre class grew by 3.6 percent and the number of farms in the 500 acres or more class grew by 9.8 percent. The main crops in Texas, cotton, sorghum, and rice, account for two thirds of total agricultural value. But the value of crops sold declined by 15.7 percent between 1964 and 1969. In sharp contrast, the sales of livestock, poultry, and their products increased by 122.8 percent. While the rate of increase of the number of tractors was only 4.7 percent between 1964 and 1969, improved technology has meant that each new piece of farm machinery is more efficient, hence more capable of displacing farm labor.

The massive displacements resulting from increasing average farm size and improved agricultural technology imply a continuing decline in agricultural employment for the foreseeable future. Because of the extent of past displacement, however, the high *rate* of decline is not expected to continue. Assuming that the *rate* of decline will be one half what it was during the 1960-1970 decade (one half of 38.2 percent), nonmetropolitan agricultural losses will amount to only about 23,400 between 1970 and 1980. This figure is clearly much less than the 75,900 of the 1960-1970 decade. The validity of the assumption that future rates of decline in agricultural employment will be lower will be made clear by comparison of the size of the predicted 1980 agricultural employment using the above rate and the actual 1960-1970 trend. The higher rate leaves only 76,000 employees in all of nonmetropolitan Texas agriculture, forestry, and fisheries, while the lower rate leaves 99,400, which seems to be a more realistic figure.

---

[8]Texas Good Neighbor Commission, *Texas Migrant Labor—Annual Report, 1970* (Austin, Texas: Texas Employment Commission, 1970), p. 2.

Chapter II

IMPLICATIONS AND IMPACT OF RURAL DEVELOPMENT

Industrialization Potential of Nonmetropolitan Texas

The nonmetropolitan areas of Texas are clearly capable of attracting industry; this is not a phenomenon only of those regions adjacent to metropolitan areas. Indeed, the nonmetropolitan areas more distant than fifty miles from a metropolitan central city had a manufacturing growth rate of 72 percent between 1959 and 1969, as compared with only 43.7 percent for metropolitan areas.[1]

The ability of nonmetropolitan Texas to attract industry can be further seen from Table 20, which shows the growth rates of industrial employment by region. Though total manufacturing in nonmetropolitan areas was growing at slower rates than that in the state as a whole, some industries grew at higher rates in nonmetropolitan areas than in the state as a whole. These include furniture and lumber, metal industries, machinery except electrical, electrical machinery, and textiles and apparel. Some sectors, however, have been declining in nonmetropolitan areas. These include transport equipment, food, and other nondurables. These mixed results suggest a need for selectivity in searching for industrial prospects for rural economic development. Industries that have been growing rapidly may find it advantageous to locate in rural areas. Further, many variations by region should be considered in deciding which industries are most likely to be attracted to an area.

---

[1]Thomas E. Till, "Rural Industrialization and Southern Rural Poverty in the 1960's: Patterns of Labor Demand in Southern Nonmetropolitan Labor Markets and Their Impact on Local Poverty," Ph.D. dissertation, The University of Texas at Austin, 1972.

Table 20

RATES OF GROWTH IN MANUFACTURING EMPLOYMENT IN NONMETROPOLITAN TEXAS, 1960-1970, BY REGION
(Percent)

Industry	East nonmetro-politan	Southwest nonmetro-politan	Northwest nonmetro-politan	Total nonmetro-politan	Total Texas
Manufacturing	26.3	9.9	10.4	22.1	35.9
Furniture and lumber	32.4	60.6	136.3	35.4	3.8
Metal industries	119.6	7.9	80.5	83.5	55.9
Machinery, except electrical	79.5	5.8	13.6	55.1	40.9
Electrical machinery	328.0	774.6	512.2	357.3	16.9
Transport equipment	− 27.1	50.5	187.2	− 19.1	93.4
Other durable goods	69.8	131.1	− 12.9	55.5	92.7
Food	− 8.7	− 19.2	− 10.2	− 12.0	− 20.3
Textiles and apparel	32.7	8.5	233.3	46.4	38.2
Printing and publishing	17.3	6.9	− 18.4	5.3	15.4
Chemicals	49.3	44.2	− 45.8	4.5	23.3
Other nondurables	− 77.9	− 10.8	− 9.3	− 36.8	19.8

Source: See statistical appendix.

While nonmetropolitan areas have had success with manufacturing growth, the "quality" of nonagricultural employment in nonmetropolitan Texas is generally below that of metropolitan areas, as may be readily seen by studying the 1970 structure of nonmetropolitan nonagricultural employment. Nonmetropolitan industrial structures are characterized by lower average earnings (see Table 21). Furthermore, relative to metropolitan Texas, the quality of nonmetropolitan industrial structures generally has been deteriorating.

The lower quality of nonmetropolitan manufacturing employment is also evident from Table 22, which presents the percentage distribution of manufacturing employment by region. Comparison of the proportion of total employment in a given industry for nonmetropolitan and metropolitan areas reveals the relative concentration of different industries in nonmetropolitan areas. Generally

Table 21

INDEXES OF INDUSTRIAL STRUCTURE*
FOR NONAGRICULTURAL EMPLOYMENT

Region	1960 Male	1960 Female	1970 Male	1970 Female
East nonmetropolitan	$6,992	$2,926	$7,140	$3,009
Southwest nonmetropolitan	7,096	2,936	6,900	3,170
Northwest nonmetropolitan	7,331	2,938	7,287	3,004
Nonmetropolitan	7,100	2,931	7,118	3,043
Metropolitan	7,270	3,056	7,412	3,210
Nonmetropolitan relative to metropolitan	97.66%	95.91%	96.04%	94.80%

* Calculated from occupational distributions, excluding farmers, farm labor, and private household workers, using 1969 U.S. male and female earnings weights.

Source: See statistical appendix.

the industries that are more heavily concentrated in nonmetropolitan areas are lower-wage, slower-growth industries. For example, 1.83 percent of nonmetropolitan employment is in furniture and lumber, while metropolitan areas have only .5 percent of their employment in these slow-growth (Column 6, Table 22) and low-wage (Column 7, Table 22) sectors. Nonmetropolitan employment is concentrated in industries that have educational requirements below the average.

The adverse concentration of industry probably is caused largely by the underemphasis on human resource development in nonmetropolitan Texas. For example, in Texas the median number of years of schooling is 10.3 for nonmetropolitan and 12.1 for metropolitan areas. In nonmetropolitan areas, only 22.8 percent of males with less than 15 years of school have completed some vocational training, as compared with 29.6 percent for metropolitan areas. If nonmetropolitan Texas is to improve the growth and income characteristics of its industrial structure, greater attention will have to be paid to development of human resources.

Table 22

PERCENTAGE DISTRIBUTION OF MANUFACTURING EMPLOYMENT, BY REGION, 1970

Industry	East nonmetro-politan (1)	Southwest nonmetro-politan (2)	Northwest nonmetro-politan (3)	Total nonmetro-politan (4)	Metropolitan (5)	1960-1970 growth rate for Texas (6)	Average weekly earnings, 1969 (7)	Median years of schooling for males (8)
Total employment	100.00	100.00	100.00	100.00	100.00	24.8	$120.16	11.1
Manufacturing	17.91	9.34	10.92	14.11	15.01	35.9	133.73	10.9
Furniture and lumber	3.28	0.29	0.29	1.83	0.54	3.8	113.04	8.6
Metal industries	3.06	1.11	0.44	1.98	2.33	55.9	151.41	10.6
Machinery, except electrical	1.57	0.25	1.02	1.09	1.90	40.9	154.95	11.6
Electrical machinery	0.82	0.18	0.12	0.50	1.84	16.9	131.27	12.3
Transport equipment	1.71	0.26	0.42	1.04	2.77	93.4	164.02	11.5
Other durable goods	1.88	0.77	0.89	1.37	1.74	92.7	128.96	10.5
Food	1.47	1.33	1.17	1.37	1.64	– 20.3	127.98	10.4
Textiles and apparel	2.01	2.09	2.57	2.15	1.24	38.2	97.76	9.2
Printing and publishing	0.81	0.54	0.73	0.72	1.32	15.4	147.78	11.6
Chemicals	1.03	0.89	1.16	1.02	1.60	23.3	153.50	12.2
Other nondurable goods	0.28	1.63	2.11	1.03	1.74	19.8	128.96	10.5

Source: See statistical appendix.

Impact and Implications of the Kinds of Industries Locating in Rural Areas

While it is desirable to upgrade the types of industries locating in nonmetropolitan areas, this effort must be accompanied by improvement in the quality of local human resources if low-income nonmetropolitan citizens with lower educational levels are not to be bypassed. Since over 37 percent of nonmetropolitan Texans have less than one year of high school, and almost 12 percent have less than five years of elementary school, importing high-skill plants will not directly benefit those whose employment opportunities are the most limited. For example, high-skill industrial development is not likely to provide employment opportunities for males who have been out of work (see regression analysis, Table A-4, statistical appendix).

High-skill industries often induce inmigration of skilled labor from metropolitan areas and therefore have little direct employment impact on the nonmetropolitan unemployed. While a certain amount of inmigration of high-skill industry and labor may be desirable for the industrial diversification of nonmetropolitan areas, low-skill industries might give the inexperienced work force the needed experience in industrial employment which can be a valuable asset in attracting higher-quality industry in the future. On the other hand, marginal industry employing workers with limited skills could portend future trouble for an area if that industry either becomes unprofitable or migrates to other areas or counties. Moreover, the regression results show that high-wage, high-skill industries have favorable impacts on incomes, poverty, labor force participation rates, and high school enrollment rates (see regression analysis, Table A-4, statistical appendix), suggesting the desirability of a balanced mix of low- and high-skill industrial development. However, high-skill industry is not likely to hire the indigenous population of an area unless that population acquires the necessary skills and education.

The favorable impact of employment growth on the occupational structure in nonmetropolitan areas can be seen from the index of occupational position in Table 21, which measures in dollars the expected earnings of the work force if the U.S. average wage were paid in each occupation. Both males and females in nonmetropolitan areas improved their earnings between 1960 and 1970, and the situation in nonmetropolitan areas improved relative to that in metropolitan areas.

The differential impacts of nonmetropolitan employment growth by occupation and sex can be seen from Tables 23, 24, and 25. Especially noteworthy is the *decline* in absolute employment for males simultaneously with the increase in employment of females. Males sustained major losses in agriculture but also lost employment as managers, operatives, private household workers, and laborers. In contrast, agricultural losses for women and their losses in private household work were more than offset by increases in other nonfarm sectors.

The simultaneous loss of almost 5,000 male operative jobs at a time when female operative employment was growing by 11,000 could be a cause for concern about the economic health of nonmetropolitan areas where men are unable to find new jobs when they are displaced from old ones. This problem also is highlighted by the projections of present trends in Tables 24 and 25. A loss of 36,619 jobs for men as farmers and farm managers, nonfarm managers, operatives, private household workers, farm laborers, and nonfarm laborers is anticipated during the 1970s. If these predictions prove accurate, nonmetropolitan male employ-

Table 23

INDEXES OF OCCUPATIONAL POSITION FOR TEXAS*

Region	1960 Male	1960 Female	1970 Male	1970 Female
Metropolitan	7,121	2,941	7,296	3,122
Nonmetropolitan	5,876	2,613	6,313	2,878
Nonmetropolitan relative to metropolitan	82.5%	88.8%	86.5%	92.2%

* Using 1969 U.S. male and female earnings weights.
Source: See statistical appendix.

Table 24

OCCUPATIONAL CHANGES FOR MALES IN NONMETROPOLITAN TEXAS, 1960-1970 AND 1970-1980

Occupation	1960	1970	Change in employment, 1960-1970	Percent change in employment, 1960-1970	Forecasted change in employment, 1970-1980
Total employment	713,522	661,348	− 52,174	− 7.3	5,125
Professional and technical	47,340	52,149	4,809	10.2	5,319
Farmers and farm managers	109,496	57,905	− 51,591	− 47.1	− 13,637
Managers	76,520	69,900	− 6,620	− 8.7	− 6,081
Clerical	29,452	33,161	3,709	12.6	4,178
Sales	34,132	36,480	2,348	6.9	2,517
Craft workers	126,061	139,695	13,634	10.8	15,087
Operatives	137,245	132,307	− 4,938	− 3.6	− 4,763
Private household	3,075	880	− 2,195	− 71.4	− 628
Service workers	31,168	42,066	10,898	3.5	14,723
Farm laborers	62,346	45,220	− 17,126	− 27.5	− 6,218
Laborers, nonfarm	56,713	50,680	− 6,033	− 10.6	− 5,372

Source: See statistical appendix.

ment will grow by only 5,125 jobs during the decade. Women, by contrast, would gain 146,501 jobs net; their losses would be confined mainly to agriculture and domestic service; and they would gain jobs in all other areas where male employment is declining.

The projections in Tables 24 and 25 are based on the assumption that the events of the past provide some guidance for the future. Specifically the forecasts assume that the 1960-1970 *rates* of change by occupation will be repeated, with the exception of agricultural employment. The farming occupations were assumed to decline at a rate equal to one half of their previous rates. Using these assumptions, the forecast is for male losses to be turned into

Table 25

OCCUPATIONAL CHANGES FOR FEMALES IN NONMETROPOLITAN TEXAS, 1960-1970 AND 1970-1980

Occupation	1960	1970	Change in employment, 1960-1970	Percent change in employment, 1960-1970	Forecasted change in employment, 1970-1980
Total employment	268,043	348,265	80,222	29.9	146,501
Professional and technical	40,449	56,615	16,166	40.0	22,646
Farmers and farm managers	4,801	2,671	– 2,130	– 44.4	– 593
Managers	14,608	15,669	1,061	7.3	1,144
Clerical	59,597	93,059	33,462	56.2	52,299
Sales	24,961	26,075	1,114	4.5	1,173
Craft workers	2,688	7,462	4,774	177.6	13,253
Operatives	25,858	37,097	11,239	43.5	16,137
Private household	37,276	26,309	– 10,967	– 29.4	– 7,735
Service workers	48,099	75,356	27,257	56.7	42,727
Farm laborers	8,123	3,926	– 4,197	– 51.7	– 1,015
Laborers, nonfarm	1,543	4,023	2,480	160.7	6,465

Source: See statistical appendix.

marginal gains and for female gains to increase. It appears likely, then, that the gap between male and female employment is likely to remain in the 1970s.

Similar results are obtained by applying the above assumptions on a regional level. While both male and female employment can be expected to increase more rapidly or decline less rapidly, the gap between male and female opportunities is expected to continue (see Tables A-5 through A-10, statistical appendix).

The projected employment changes vary considerably between regions, but the general conclusion of losses for men and gains for women holds. The greatest gains for men are expected in East Texas, where men are projected to have a net gain of 41,333 jobs.

The greatest projected gains for men are 19,294 craft worker and 9,973 professional and technical jobs; the losses are confined to agriculture and domestic service. Women in East Texas are projected to gain over twice as many jobs net as men—90,690; the major projected gains for women are 35,492 clerical, 28,800 service, and 13,365 operative jobs. Projected female losses in East Texas are restricted to agriculture and domestic household work (see statistical appendix, Tables A-5 and A-6).

In the southwest and northwest, males are expected to suffer net job losses of 7,329 and 17,626, respectively. In the southwest, the main losses are expected to occur in the following occupational categories: operatives, 3,987; farmers and farm managers, 3,500; managers, 3,355; and farm laborers, 2,861 (see statistical appendix, Table A-7).

Women in the southwest are expected to gain 49,382 jobs, mainly in these four categories: craft workers, 14,248 jobs; professional and technical workers, 14,046 jobs; clerical workers, 11,461 jobs; and service workers, 8,352 jobs (see Table A-8, statistical appendix).

The greatest regional net loss for males is in the northwest, where men are expected to lose 17,672 jobs and women are expected to gain 18,378 jobs. According to these projections, men would continue to lose jobs in every category except services, with the greatest losses in agriculture (which, nonetheless, will not be as numerous as the 13,197 farmer and farm manager and 996 farm laborer jobs lost in this region between 1960 and 1970), operatives, and managers. Women in the northwest are projected to continue to make major gains in service, professional and technical, and clerical jobs, and smaller gains in craft worker, operative, and nonfarm laborer categories (see Tables A-9 and A-10, statistical appendix).

Effects of Commuting Patterns and Migration on Labor Supply

A thorough analysis of the effect of commuting patterns and migration on labor supplies requires a great deal more information than is currently available. It is known, however, that in nonmetropolitan areas in which less than 10 percent of the labor force commuted to jobs across county lines in 1960, the extent of subemployment (as defined earlier) was significantly higher than in other nonmetropolitan counties in 1970. Thus the extent of job commuting opportunities apparently has a large impact upon the success of labor market participants in rural areas. Viewed from a different perspective, the quality of employment opportunities shapes the decision to commute.

The relatively better educated and younger Texans have been migrating out of rural areas. Such migration has severe implications for the quality of the remaining labor supply and community leadership in rural areas and partly explains the relatively high nonmetropolitan dependency ratios in Table 4. Even with the flight from rural areas, the incomes of those remaining have not improved—a phenomenon at least partially explained by the deteriorating demand conditions in rural areas.

Nonmetropolitan Texas "turned around" in the 1960s and experienced a population growth. Population growth, however, is not entirely desirable in labor surplus areas. Particular attention must be paid to the characteristics of the individuals who accounted for the growth and where, precisely, the growth took place. Until this is known, the impact on labor supply cannot be anticipated.

In Texas, as in the nation, population changes do not necessarily reflect employment changes. Moreover, population does not necessarily grow in the places with the tightest labor markets. Indeed, in Texas, there apparently existed an *inverse* relationship between subemployment and population change, as indicated by the following statistics:

Region	*Subemployment (males, 1970)*	*Size of change in population, 1960-1970*
East	25.1	26.0%
Southwest	22.7	7.2%
Northwest	15.2	− 6.1%
Metropolitan	11.8	23.8%

Although a great deal of individual commuting and moving may have taken place in Texas owing to labor market factors, labor supply growth and subemployment are still found in the same areas.

Rural Development and Protective Legislation

Nonagricultural labor in rural areas has the benefit of all protective legislation that applies to metropolitan employees. This legislation, however, may have a differential impact on employees of nonagricultural establishments in rural areas. To some extent the problem in serving rural areas is an administrative one. Administration is more difficult in sparsely populated regions; in addition, since there are fewer workers' organizations to police the administration of these measures, violations probably are higher than in urban areas.

Agricultural labor, in contrast to the nonfarm labor force, is covered hardly at all by protective legislation.[2] Although it has been argued that minimum wages in agriculture will speed mechanization and expand unemployment, the evidence is not entirely clear. Nationally, mechanization and consequent declines in employment have been more rapid in those agricultural enterprises not covered by minimum wage laws than in those most affected by those measures. Furthermore, if wages are raised in agriculture, the work force may be stabilized, along with per unit labor costs, as more capable employees decide to postpone their flight from the agricultural labor force. Far from being antiemployer, minimum wage legislation may actually help employers by reducing the intensity of wage competition for qualified employees.

Since compensation for work-related accidents is primarily a function of the states rather than the federal government, Texas obviously has a role to play in promoting more liberal workmen's compensation coverage. To date, Texas has neglected to extend coverage to agricultural workers; even under recent Texas legisla-

[2]In 1966 minimum wage coverage was extended to about 2 percent of the nation's farms, which employed about half of the hired farm work force and two thirds of the migrants.

tion, farm and ranch employers are not required to have accident insurance. As with minimum wages, the impact could be important in maintaining a high-quality agricultural work force. Further, the protection offered by workmen's compensation is now needed in agriculture because increased mechanization has made farm work more hazardous. The National Commission on State Workmen's Compensation Laws recommends:

> As of July 1, 1973, coverage should be extended to agricultural employees whose employer's annual payroll exceeds $1,000. By July 1, 1975, coverage should be extended to farm workers on the same basis as all employees.

Another aspect of protective legislation in which the state can be active is the expansion of unemployment insurance. There seem to be no impelling economic arguments against the expansion of unemployment insurance and several strong economic, social, and moral reasons for expanding coverage to the agricultural sector.

The seasonal nature of agricultural employment has often been used as an argument against the use of unemployment insurance in the agricultural sector. Seasonality is decreasing, however, and other industries, such as construction, with significant seasonal components have long been covered.

Moreover, even if a large number of interstate seasonal workers are included in coverage, the maximum subsidy of the nonagricultural sector to agriculture in Texas would be $.07 per $1,000 of taxable earnings. Under such conditions of coverage, using current coverage criteria, 92 percent of employers and 99 percent of gross payroll would be covered.[3] In a thorough study at Texas A&M University of the financial implications of extending unemployment insurance to agriculture, Fritsch, Nergart, and Ruesink conclude:

> The overall effect on the Texas state benefits/taxable wages ratio due to inclusion of the agricultural sector under unemployment insurance legislation would be minimal. . . . On the average, the agricultural sector would be

---

[3]Conrad Fritsch, Karen F. Nergart, and David C. Ruesink, *Extension of Unemployment Insurance to Agriculture* (College Station, Texas: Texas A&M University in conjunction with Regional Research Project NE-58 of the Northeast Agricultural Experiment Station, 1973).

self-financing although the actual ratio of benefits as a proportion of taxable wages would be above the four percent maximum state rate for some employers. Even under the unlikely hypothetical event that all agricultural employers would experience benefit/taxable wages ratios as high as 7 percent, the added cost to nonagricultural employers would have been less than seven hundredths of one percent of taxable wages.[4]

Thus it appears economically feasible to provide agricultural workers with unemployment insurance, a form of security that most nonfarm workers have enjoyed for decades.

In conclusion, improved and expanded application of protective legislation—minimum wage law, workmen's compensation, and unemployment insurance—in rural areas is not only feasible but desirable, for it will enhance the competitive position of rural employers to better maintain a high-quality work force.

[4] *Ibid.*, p. 40.

Chapter III

RURAL MANPOWER PROGRAMS

Since rural manpower programs are designed to improve the operation of labor markets and upgrade the productivity of workers, they have important implications for rural development. Because of the special problems of rural areas, however, urban manpower programs cannot simply be transferred, unaltered, to rural areas. Rural labor markets differ from those of urban areas in being less concentrated geographically, having fewer labor market organizations and institutions, placing greater reliance on informal labor market information systems, having different industry structures (that is, more low-wage, labor-intensive activities; more agricultural, less professional-technical and white-collar employment; and more competitive industries), and providing fewer alternatives to the buyers and sellers of labor.

The effectiveness of rural labor markets is important for all groups in rural areas and for the state as a whole. Better job opportunities will help hold people in rural areas, thereby lessening the problems of congested urban areas and slowing down the rate of rural decay. Moreover, the operation of labor markets is important for employers as well as workers. Few businesses can be successful without dependable supplies of qualified workers. Indeed, a problem of growing concern for rural employers is the fact that inadequate incomes and alternatives cause the most productive workers to leave rural areas.

Because of its importance for rural development, the subject of the effectiveness of rural manpower programs deserves close attention. This chapter, therefore, explores efforts to develop rural manpower programs and discusses some rural manpower problems.

More detailed discussions of some rural manpower programs in Texas are provided in an appendix.

An important economic problem for rural Texas is how to provide higher incomes and better employment opportunities for the unemployed or underemployed and how to facilitate the movement of people from labor surplus areas to sites where jobs are more plentiful. Manpower programs clearly cannot solve all the problems of rural areas, but they could play an important role in both the process of industrialization and the movement of people to places where job opportunities exist. Manpower programs could facilitate industrialization by providing potential employers with information about local labor markets, helping employers train their work forces, and providing training for unemployed workers or upgrading training for those who are employed. Indeed, federal agencies have a number of programs designed to facilitate the use of manpower in economic development, and some states have made manpower an integral part of their industrial development activities because they realize that the kinds of firms attracted to their states are strongly influenced by the quality of potential work forces. Higher income paying firms are likely to be attracted by educated and trained work forces.

The main rural manpower institution has been the U.S. Employment Service, which traditionally has concentrated on meeting the seasonal labor requirements of employers and has done little to help farm workers acquire nonfarm jobs as the demand for agricultural labor declines. In order to become more effective in rural areas, the U.S. Department of Labor (DOL) created the Rural Manpower Service (RMS) in 1971. The immediate aim of the RMS was to use existing staff more effectively in providing "equity of access" to manpower services for all groups in rural areas. The equity of access strategy is concerned with the problems of achieving equitable allocations of resources for rural people, the development of specialized programs to deal with spatial and other problems involved in extending manpower and other services to rural populations, the development of cooperative arrangements with other rural agencies, and the restructuring and reorienting of the RMS to attain these goals.

Even after the creation of the RMS, however, the delivery of rural manpower services was limited by inadequate funds, the frequent isolation of the former farm labor specialist from the mainstream of rural manpower activities, and the inflexibility of the local employment office organizational structure. The RMS is therefore experimenting with three pilot projects to improve the delivery of rural manpower services.

Operation Hitchhike is attempting to attach manpower programs to existing rural institutions in order to reach scattered rural populations more effectively. There were fourteen such projects across the nation in September 1972. This approach is based on the assumption that it is more difficult to build new manpower delivery mechanisms than to utilize existing agencies like the Agricultural Extension Service, Chamber of Commerce, and the Farmers Union. Efforts to establish a hitchhike program in Texas failed, but these programs are under way in nine states.

The *Ottumwa Plan*, or *Area Concept Expansion* (ACE) program, which seeks to link central manpower service centers with feeder units reaching into the hinterland but drawing on the expertise of the central office, gives considerable promise of meeting some of the problems involved in delivering manpower services to thinly populated rural areas. This approach was developed in the Ottumwa, Iowa, area, where four offices serving twelve counties were reorganized to form a unified approach to the whole area. This program was in operation in twelve states in fiscal 1972 and had demonstrated its effectiveness in eliminating duplication and enlarging the services available to rural residents. There is no ACE program in Texas, although the Texas Employment Commission has twenty-two rural suboffices and nine itinerant employment offices in rural areas.

The *National Migrant Worker Program* (NMWP) is designed to make it possible for migrants to leave the migrant stream. To accomplish this, the NMWP attempts to provide a comprehensive program of manpower and supportive services to enable the migrant to secure permanent year-round employment that will provide an income above the poverty level. In fiscal 1971-1972, the DOL earmarked $20.5 million in MDTA funds to provide services for 5,800 migrants and their families. The NMWP is particularly important in Texas, because many migrants to other parts of the country originate there. (For further discussion of manpower programs for migrants, see Appendix A.)

In addition, the DOL has a number of ongoing rural manpower pilot projects. One of these is the *Smaller Communities Program*, operating in nineteen states. Under this program, traveling teams of specialists carry manpower services into rural areas. In Texas, the Texas Employment Commission has a Smaller Communities team of five specialists. While this program provides useful services to local areas, its effectiveness is reduced because of the itinerant and intermittent nature of the services provided.

Although training programs have not been very effective in rural areas, primarily because of inadequate training facilities, rural workers have participated in a number of regular manpower programs. In fiscal 1970, for example, 250,000 people in rural counties were enrolled in work experience and training programs. Most of these enrollees were in *Neighborhood Youth Corps* (NYC) programs, which could be a major vehicle for easing the rural-to-urban transition, since the majority of the rural youth will be migrating and in need of assistance. In nonmetropolitan Texas, NYC programs had 264 out-of-school slots in fiscal 1964; information on in-school programs was not available (see Table 26). More people can participate in each of these programs than indicated by the number of "slots" available, because several people can fill a given slot during the year. Nationally, *institutional* and *on-the-job training MDTA programs* enrolled only about 42,000 rural people in 1970, and few of these were trained for expanding skilled farm jobs. Clearly, to be effective, these programs need to provide training as well as jobs.

Rural workers participated in a number of other manpower programs during fiscal 1970. About 14,000 trainees in forty-five states participated in *MDTA programs linked to economic development projects* in chronic labor surplus areas. About 8,400 adult men were enrolled in *Operation Mainstream* (OM), designed to give meaningful work experience in public works to unemployed older workers. As of March 1972, OM programs operated in every state except Delaware. Because OM concentrated on meaningful work in community maintenance and beautification and did not challenge community power structures, it seems to have been a fairly successful work program, although it provided limited skill training and upgrading opportunities and did little to get its participants absorbed into private employment. Operation Mainstream has been

Table 26

DISTRIBUTIONS OF SLOTS AND FUNDS TO MANPOWER PROGRAMS*
IN METROPOLITAN AND NONMETROPOLITAN TEXAS, FISCAL 1973

Program*	State totals		Metropolitan		Nonmetropolitan	
	Slots	Funds	Slots	Funds	Slots	Funds
Public Service Careers (PSC)*	876	$ 1,666,780	876	$ 1,666,780	0	None
Work Incentive (WIN)**	3,400	8,565,312	3,350	8,389,251	50	$ 176,061
Concentrated Employment Program (CEP)	7,427	10,420,618	6,527	8,969,638	900	1,450,980
National Migrant Worker Program (NMWP)	1,517	4,870,300	n.a.	n.a.	n.a.	n.a.
Operation Mainstream (OM)**	766	2,953,610	185	713,340	581	2,240,270
Neighborhood Youth Corps (NYC)						
In school	11,308	7,523,065	n.a.	n.a.	n.a.	n.a.
Out of school**	1,628	5,259,741	1,364	4,387,941	264	871,800
Summer	n.a.	n.a.	n.a.	n.a.	n.a.	n.a.
New Careers	105	1,454,000	105	1,454,000	0	None
Job Opportunities in the Business Sector (JOBS)†	6,727	12,338,460	6,013	11,270,969	714	1,067,491
JOPS (JOBS optional)	1,200	1,205,304	n.a.	n.a.	n.a.	n.a.
Project SER	1,936	4,122,433	1,936	4,122,433	0	None
Opportunities Industrialization Center (OIC)	1,107	1,081,239	1,107	1,081,239	0	None
Model Cities Manpower and Job Development	n.a.	2,900,320	n.a.	2,871,320	n.a.	29,000
MDTA Institutional	2,890	6,654,000				
Vocational Education††						
Secondary	317,656	n.a.	197,078	n.a.	120,578	n.a.
Postsecondary	88,368	n.a.	80,163	n.a.	8,205	n.a.
Adult secondary	141,808	n.a.	110,961	n.a.	30,847	n.a.

* See manpower appendix for brief description of programs.
** Figures involve interpolation.
† Fiscal year 1972.
†† 1971-1972 scholastic year.
Source: Interviews with Texas Employment Commission and state manpower planning office.

a fairly effective program in Texas, although it had only 581 slots in the state during fiscal 1973 and apparently is scheduled to be phased out as a national program. However, the program could be continued under manpower revenue sharing.

Another program designed specifically to help rural people is the *Concerted Services in Training and Education* (CSTE) project, which is defined as

a pilot effort to improve smaller communities and rural areas by demonstrating that education and occupational training, in conjunction with other economic development activities, can significantly help to increase employment opportunities.

CSTE was suggested by a Cabinet-level rural development committee and organized by a sixteen-member task force. CSTE seeks to develop means for concentrating interagency resources on the

Table 27

ESTIMATED NUMBER OF ENROLLEES IN URBAN AND RURAL WORK AND TRAINING PROGRAMS ADMINISTERED BY THE U.S. DEPARTMENT OF LABOR, FISCAL 1970
(In thousands)

Program	Estimated enrollment, FY 1970	Urban areas		Rural areas	
		Number	Percent of enrollees	Number	Percent of enrollees
Total	1,051.4	799.9	76	251.5	24
Manpower Development and Training					
Institutional	130.0	105.3	81	24.7	19
On the job	91.0	73.7	81	17.3	19
Neighborhood Youth Corps					
In school	74.4	43.2	58	31.2	42
Out of school	46.2	31.9	69	14.3	31
Summer	361.5	245.8	68	115.7	32
Operation Mainstream	12.5	4.1	33	8.4	67
Public Service Careers (New Careers)	3.6	3.2	89	.4	11
Concentrated Employment Program	110.1	98.0	89	12.1	11
JOBS (federally financed)	86.8	86.8	100	0	0
Work Incentive Program	92.7	74.2	80	18.5	20
Job Corps	42.6	33.7	79	8.9	21

Source: Office of Manpower Management Data Systems, Manpower Administration, U.S. Department of Labor.

problems of people in selected communities; identify employment opportunities and occupational education programs for the poor and unemployed; develop ways in which rural communities can promote human resource development; demonstrate the potential of human resource development programs to improve employment opportunities; and demonstrate the value of local involvement in human resource development programs. In order to accomplish these objectives, seventeen CSTE pilot projects had been established in thirteen states, including Texas, by the end of fiscal 1971. CSTE is based on the assumption that many available resources in rural areas fail to be utilized because of fragmentation and lack of leadership to coordinate various developmental efforts. The CSTE agent therefore seeks to bring these resources together and provide the catalyst for developmental programs. Evaluations of this program conclude that these assumptions are justified, but the programs are not extensive enough and have not been in operation long enough to have had much tangible impact on rural employment and incomes. (A CSTE program in Red River County, Texas, is analyzed in Appendix A.) This concept clearly has considerable promise as a rural development vehicle in Texas.

There also were thirteen rural *Concentrated Employment Programs* (CEPs) in 1970, one of which was in Eagle Pass, Texas. Although there is some controversy about the effectiveness of the rural CEPs in achieving their objective of concentrating a variety of manpower resources in order to improve the job opportunities of poor people in rural areas, a national evaluation of five rural CEPs concluded that they had improved the employment and incomes of their participants. The programs clearly were popular with their participants, who not only obtained better and more stable jobs but also improved their levels of living markedly. The rural CEPs also demonstrated considerable flexibility in adjusting to the diverse training, economic development, and work experience realities in their areas. This adaptability was necessary because the basic CEP concept was designed for concentrated urban populations, not for scattered target groups in a number of political entities in rural areas. However, interviewees at the Texas Employment Commission do not consider the Eagle Pass CEP an effective manpower organization.

Rural governments also have participated in the *Public Service Careers* (PSC) and *Emergency Employment Act* (EEA) programs, designed to open government jobs to the unemployed and disadvantaged. Since many government programs operate in rural areas, public employment offers considerable promise as a means of providing employment. However, these programs have been limited because few rural governments have merit systems (which are required for PSC participation) or personnel to administer the programs.

Rural participation in EEA programs, in Texas and in the nation, has been limited because the allocation formula (unemployment) used by the EEA discriminates against rural areas and because the EEA's framers were not sufficiently sensitive to the unique problems of rural areas (see Appendix A). Although rural areas have been disadvantaged by the act, they have benefited from provisions which give funds to Indians on reservations, migrant workers, and counties with a population of 75,000 or less (by March 1972, rural counties had received 29 percent of the funds allocated under this section). Nevertheless, if restructured, public employment programs, together with an expansion of Operation Mainstream-type programs, could provide jobs for the unemployed and underemployed in rural areas, many of whom are unlikely to be absorbed by private employment without generating an economic expansion so large as to cause intense inflation.

The Public Employment Program (PEP) in Texas

Comparative data show that PEP is clearly no substitute for OM in reaching the rural disadvantaged (see Appendix A). Data on PEP and Operation Mainstream for 1972 reveal that 42 percent of OM enrollees and only 9 percent of PEP enrollees had eight years or less of school. At the other end of the scale, only 3 percent of OM enrollees, but 32 percent of PEP enrollees, had at least some college. Nationally, 73 percent of OM enrollees and 24 percent of PEP participants had less than a high school education. The same trend is evident at the state level: 43 percent of Texas PEP enrollees had some college, while less than .5 percent of OM enrollees attended college. If education is a good measure of disadvantage, Operation Mainstream apparently serves a much larger proportion of disadvantaged workers.

It would be more equitable to compare the PEP "balance of state"[1] with OM in Texas. Cumulative enrollment figures for the first nine months of PEP in Texas' "balance of state" support the conclusion that PEP was not so concerned as OM with disadvantaged workers. About 24 percent of OM enrollees in Texas had eight years or less of education, whereas only about 12 percent of the PEP "balance of state" enrollees were in the same group. Almost 60 percent of PEP "balance of state," but only 22 percent of OM participants, had twelve or more years of school. Only a fraction of 1 percent of Texas OM enrollees had any education beyond high school, while 18.7 percent of the PEP "balance of state" enrollees had some college.

According to PEP's definition, 33.1 percent of the Texas "balance of state" enrollees were "disadvantaged." Virtually all OM enrollees were disadvantaged by the same definition.

According to the preliminary reports on the "balance of state," 300 out of 1,500 Texas PEP enrollees have been permanently placed. In contrast, the OM program with the best placement record placed about two thirds of all terminees. OM has apparently creamed* less and has probably done as well or better in permanently placing enrollees, although the Green Thumb program, which caters mainly to older workers, does not have as good a placement record as PEP. Finally, the PEP program cost approximately $7,000 per enrollee, much higher than the cost for OM, which in Texas was $1,780 per enrollee.

*Here "creaming" means skimming off the best workers.

[1]"Balance of state" is the geographic area outside the political jurisdiction of other designated program agents participating in PEP. These latter designated agents are primarily cities or counties of over 75,000 population that are directly funded. The "balance of state" is a residual consisting of smaller towns and rural areas. "Balance of state" funds are administered through the Department of Community Affairs, Office of the Governor, State of Texas.

The Role of Relocation Assistance in a Rural Human Resource Development Policy

Many economic development experts believe migration to be the most effective remedy for the problems of rural labor surpluses. Migration is necessary, according to these economists, because continuing technological change in agriculture reduces jobs faster than industrialization creates them. There is therefore substantial outmigration from rural areas, especially during periods of full employment in the national economy. The potential gains of the typical mover apparently outweigh the pecuniary costs of moving. Some migrants, however, suffer income losses when they move, and many return to rural areas. There is considerable evidence of high noneconomic costs in moving that cannot be quantified.

A number of problems associated with these "natural" migration patterns, especially poor information, are generally considered by labor market analysts to be important deterrents to mobility. Other impediments to rural-urban migration are imposed by various labor market and social constraints. For example, workers with limited skills and education cannot easily break into other than marginal nonfarm jobs, particularly when skilled workers are unemployed and workers with higher levels of education are available. The returns to migration apparently outweigh the costs only for younger, better-educated workers who remain in nonfarm work long enough to acquire some job experience. Although they apparently gain considerably as compared with their situation in rural Texas, blacks and Chicanos who migrate to urban areas also face the problem of racial and cultural discrimination by employers and other labor market institutions. Finally, in calculating the returns to mobility, we must deduct the negative effects on the areas losing population. These include declining land values, deteriorating tax bases for towns, declining levels of education and skill, increasing dependency rates, and losses of the most productive labor supplies.

Because natural migration patterns have not been sufficient to reduce surplus populations in many rural areas, there is considerable support for relocation programs as alternatives to fruitless attempts to attract industry to rural areas with little economic potential, transfer payments, or a continuation of the economically "irrational" migration patterns based mainly on friends, relatives, and other contacts rather than on availability of good job opportunities. Those who favor "growth center strategies" advocate programs to rationalize the labor market by moving people to these growth centers rather than leaving workers free to migrate to congested urban areas.

As a consequence of this reasoning, the MDTA provided for a number of relocation assistance projects, which afford some insight into the effectiveness of this strategy. These pilot projects moved some 14,000 unemployed and underemployed workers and their families, mainly from rural areas, between 1965 and 1969, at a cost of about $800 per family, including about $300 for moving and settling in. These projects were generally regarded as successful in moving the unemployed and underemployed to new jobs, where most of them stayed for at least 60 days. Moreover, these programs made it possible to isolate some key factors facilitating mobility, including (1) the need for a wide range of supportive services and (2) the value of tying relocatees to specific jobs before they are relocated. Although no complete evaluation has been made, the available evidence suggests that the returns to *successful* moves more than offset the costs. Many of those who were relocated, however, returned to their original home areas within a year. A complete evaluation must include the costs of these unsuccessful moves as well as the successful ones.

Furthermore, it is not clear that these relocation projects helped people who would not have moved without relocation assistance. Preliminary examination of the results suggests that most of those who were moved probably would have moved anyway and that many of those who would not have moved without help returned to rural areas. Probably, therefore, the relocation projects did more to influence the timing and direction of moves than to increase their number. Moreover, the relocation projects greatly improved the job information available to relocatees. However, the projects did little to increase the education or skill levels of disadvantaged workers.

One of the most widely publicized relocation projects moved over 600 workers from the Rio Grande Valley to the LTV plant in Grand Prairie, near Dallas. Despite careful selection and training of the workers to be moved, and a high retention rate (93 percent) after sixty days, probably fewer than 10 percent of these workers are still working at LTV and over half have returned to the valley. Moreover, many of these relocatees lost their jobs when LTV lost defense contracts. This effort has not been completely analyzed, but a study of another project to move Mexican American workers from South Texas to the Panhandle found similar heavy rates of back-movement. Personal reasons, which formed no patterns, appeared to be mainly responsible for the low retention rate.

A major obstacle to the extension of the relocation projects after 1969 on a national basis was political opposition from officials who were reluctant to see potential voters and taxpayers move out of their districts. There also was some concern about the adverse effects on the places from which more productive workers were being moved. Congress therefore did not appropriate separate funds for these projects after 1969, but the U.S. Department of Labor carried out several projects thereafter with regular MDTA experimental and demonstration funds.

Although relocation projects are not likely to be panaceas for the problems of rural Texas, they can play a role, along with other manpower programs, in helping to counteract labor market imperfections. Clearly, however, these programs complement and do not substitute for other manpower programs.

The Start-Up Training Concept

The start-up training concept is designed to overcome some of the main weaknesses of traditional manpower and vocational training programs, namely, the absence of jobs for people who have been trained, the difficulties in gearing training precisely to the needs of employers, and the fact that prospective employers often encounter considerable uncertainty concerning the availability of qualified workers in places where they contemplate establishing plants. The start-up concept attempts to minimize these problems by using training as an inducement to industrialization; it is based on the assumption that high-wage industry can be induced to hire workers in a particular place only if those workers possess the skills to give them the productivity to command higher wages. Under this concept, the employer's prospective work force is carefully selected and trained before the plant opens. The relevancy of the training can be assured by having it supervised by the plant's prospective supervisory personnel, who can be hired by the state as instructors for this purpose.

Although the Center for the Study of Human Resources at the University of Texas is undertaking a thorough evaluation of start-up training in those states where it is in operation, the results of that evaluation are not available at this writing. The experience of South Carolina, however, which has conducted a program that many observers regard as ideal, is described in an appendix.

Table 28

PERCENTAGE DISTRIBUTION OF SLOTS AND FUNDS TO MANPOWER PROGRAMS IN NONMETROPOLITAN TEXAS, FISCAL 1973

Program	Percent of slots in rural areas	Percent of funds in rural areas
Public Service Careers (PSC)	0	0
Work Incentive (WIN)	1.47	2.06
Operation Mainstream (OM)	75.85	75.85
Concentrated Employment		
Program (CEP)	12.12	13.92
Neighborhood Youth Corps (NYC)		
Out of school	16.22	16.58
New Careers	0	0
Job Opportunities in the		
Business Sector (JOBS)	10.61	8.65
Project SER	0	0
Opportunities Industrialization		
Center (OIC)	0	0
Model Cities Manpower		
and Job Development	n.a.	1.00
Vocational Education		
Secondary	37.96	n.a.
Postsecondary	9.29	n.a.
Adult secondary	21.75	n.a.

Source: See Table 26.

Rural Manpower Programs in Texas

Table 28 gives data on the allocation of funds and training slots for various manpower programs in Texas. With inclusion of vocational education programs in these totals, nonmetropolitan areas receive 28.4 percent of the training *slots*. If vocational education programs are excluded, rural areas receive only 10.5 percent of the slots for which data make possible a metropolitan-nonmetropolitan allocation. The discrepancy is even greater in the case of *funds* expended. Nonmetropolitan areas received 8.21 percent of the funds expended on the programs (see Table 26); this amounts to an expenditure of $8.67 per capita in metropolitan areas and only $1.94 per capita in nonmetropolitan areas. Table 29 reveals a similar pattern with respect to the nation as a whole; while the nonmetropolitan universe of need represents about one third of the total, less than one fourth of the enrollees are in nonmetropolitan areas.

Figures for all human resource development outlays in nonmetropolitan areas of Texas are unavailable, but they probably

Table 29

FEDERAL HUMAN RESOURCE PROGRAM EXPENDITURES IN NONMETROPOLITAN AREAS, FISCAL 1969
(In millions of dollars)

Program	Actual	If proportional to population	Gap
Health facilities construction	155	169	14
Health services and care	808	1,092	284
Elementary and secondary education	844	787	– 57
Higher and science education	377	436	59
Vocational education and manpower training	196	316	120
Total	2,380	2,800	420

Source: *Locational Analysis of Federal Expenditures in Fiscal Year 1969*, Evaluation Division, Office of Management and Budget, September 1, 1970.

follow the national pattern (see Table 29). Only in the categories of elementary and secondary education did rural areas receive an equitable share of these expenditures. The relatively large nonmetropolitan share of elementary and secondary education expenditures probably reflects the greater cost of education per student in rural areas. Rural schools are particularly likely to incur large expenditures for school buses, which do little directly to increase educational attainment.

The reasons for the inequitable distribution of human resource funds in rural areas are not clear, but they undoubtedly include the greater visibility (not necessarily severity) of urban problems, the fact that urban people are better organized politically, and the absence of agencies to administer human resource programs in rural areas.

It is difficult to specify a method to achieve equity of access. First, since the total mix of rural human resource development needs is different from that of urban areas, no fixed quota for each type of program can be specified. Moreover, it is difficult to establish need criteria. There are no good relative cost estimates for urban and rural areas, although it undoubtedly is more costly to deliver services in rural areas. Some formula allocation is necessary, however, because rural areas do not have sufficient organization and cohesive leadership to ensure equitable allocation through the processes now being used. We therefore have devised an allocation formula that might be used for this purpose (see Chapter IV). However, rather than formula allocations it probably would be better to have separate appropriations and a separate manpower system for rural areas.

Summary and Conclusions

Because most manpower training programs have been designed on a metropolitan model, rural areas have not benefited to a comparable extent. There are few occupations in rural areas for which the manpower needs are great enough to justify the establishment of training courses with twenty or thirty trainees.[2] With the exception of public service employment programs, such as NYC and OM, which may or may not include training or job transition provisions, rural areas must rely primarily upon individual referral or on-the-job training (OJT) slots.

Individual referral of trainees to an established training course somewhere in the state is expensive relative to the cost of other programs. If individual referral is relied on to a great degree, given the lower per capita expenditures in rural areas, few people will benefit from manpower expenditures. From a cost-effectiveness standpoint, OJT is a much more palatable alternative in rural areas. However, OJT relies to a much greater extent on effective information and delivery systems, and rural areas do not share equally in job-matching facilities. Moreover, many employers are deterred from participating in OJT programs because of excessive paperwork. These programs could be improved by reduction of the "red tape" for employers.

Direct U.S. Department of Labor funds, in the current federal system, cannot be used to maintain an employment service in markets with less than 10,000 in the labor force. As a result, the Texas Employment Commission, upon the recommendation of the Rural Manpower Service, has established twenty-two suboffices and nine itinerant employment offices in rural areas, supported only by technical assistance and occasional visits from the central offices. Much of the activity is funded and operated in and with the facilities of local chambers of commerce, county judges, or farm bureaus. It is highly unlikely that federal funds adequate to operate such offices will become available.

The state must rely upon the successful application of special programs such as Operation Hitchhike or supply local communities with technical assistance and start-up funds for wholly community-operated employment offices.[3] Assistance from the state in the establishment, maintenance, and use of regional job banks (such as the job bank currently in operation in Midland) would also be

---

[2]Farm operator training has been attempted, but the differential in pre- and post-training earnings was so small as to generate little enthusiasm within the project. The success of manpower programs may rest to some degree, therefore, on sufficient protective legislation.

[3]Although the Texas Muncipal League has promoted this idea, communities are reluctant because of the anticipated costs.

helpful, for rural labor markets could be improved significantly by better information.

If manpower programs, including vocational education, are to realize their significant rural development potential in Texas, a number of changes must be made. Vocational education should relate more closely to the needs of nonfarm as well as agricultural employment and should place greater emphasis on adult education and training. There is a special need for programs for rural adult Texans who wish education at the high school level. Vocational and manpower programs need to be coordinated at both state and local levels.

Manpower programs are needed by present and prospective workers and employers in rural areas. Because of their rapid displacement from rural jobs, special attention should be given to the employment needs of males and young workers who are forced to migrate because of inadequate employment opportunities. Programs particularly relevant to rural Texas include Operation Mainstream, Operation Hitchhike, the Neighborhood Youth Corps (out of school), CSTE, the National Migrant Worker Program, and start-up training. All of these should either be adopted on an experimental basis or, where success has been demonstrated, be enlarged. The NYC and Operation Mainstream programs, however, probably would be more effective if they were combined and all age restrictions were removed.

Finally, to accomplish all of these objectives, measures must be taken to ensure equity of access to human resource development resources for rural areas.

Chapter IV

SUMMARY, CONCLUSIONS, AND RECOMMENDATIONS

With some exceptions, Texas is following national patterns with respect to rural development and rural problems. The basic trend in Texas and the nation has been the displacement of people from agriculture over an extended period of time, primarily because of increasing productivity in agriculture, which has greatly reduced labor requirements. Since many of those who have been displaced are not prepared by experience, training, or education for nonfarm jobs, they remain unemployed or underemployed in rural areas or take low-wage jobs in rural or urban areas. Moreover, migration out of rural areas has left behind a "residual" population with relatively fewer people in prime working-age groups, with consequently lower per capita income. Poverty statistics show that 26 percent of the nonmetropolitan population are poor as compared with 17 percent in metropolitan areas. These statistics indicate that poverty is heavily concentrated in rural areas. However, the extent to which the conditions of rural people compare with those of urban people in Texas is not known, because we know little about differential living costs, the availability of facilities, goods, and services from land, and housing ownership, all of which supplement measured income levels.

Although the farm population is only about one sixth of the rural population of Texas, agriculture is much more important than this relatively small number suggests because agriculture is a basic historical cause of many rural problems. Many rural nonfarm industries are related to agriculture, and farming interests are stronger politically than this number implies. Moreover, while the agricultural population and labor force have declined, the rural nonfarm population and labor force have increased, but not enough to prevent the decline of the total rural population from 3,503,435 to 2,261,474 between 1960 and 1970. The rural nonfarm work force, however, increased slightly (2.9 percent). While Texas' agricultural work force was declining by over 100,000 during the 1960-1970 period, nonfarm employment grew enough to offset this drop in farm employment and provide a net increase of about 28,000 jobs. Table 30 demonstrates the distribution of farm and nonfarm employment in nonmetropolitan Texas.

Table 30

LABOR FORCE AND EMPLOYMENT IN NONMETROPOLITAN TEXAS, 1970

Total population	2,912,659
Civilian labor force	1,050,018
Total employment	1,009,573
Nonfarm employment	895,236
Farm employment	114,337
Farmers and farm managers	62,095
Farm laborers and farm foremen	52,242

Source: See statistical appendix.

Behind these aggregate changes, however, lie specific developments. Agriculture is an important source of income and employment in Texas and is likely to remain so in the future. Indeed, there are some indications that the state's agriculture is becoming economically more competitive for resources with nonagricultural activities, and this trend is likely to continue. If this happens, the incomes and working conditions of farmers and their employees will improve. In Texas and in the nation, the average size of farms is increasing, and farms are becoming more land- and capital-intensive and less labor-intensive.

Though these general trends in agriculture are fairly clear, the factors responsible for the trends and their implications for the development of human resources are not clear. It is not known, for example, to what extent the displacement of people from agriculture is due to considerations of economic efficiency and to what extent it results from U.S. agricultural and tax policies favoring larger corporate farms at the expense of family farms.

U.S. agricultural policies seem generally to favor large farmers over smaller ones, and U.S. tax policy has made it attractive for nonagricultural corporations to invest in land and engage in agricultural activities in competition with family farmers who lack the corporations' nonagricultural tax advantages. The influence of these considerations on the displacement of smaller farmers has not been determined. Moreover, the changing character of agricultural employment necessitates greater attention to the conditions of agricultural workers. Clearly, therefore, agriculture must receive considerable attention in any rural human resource development strategy.

Disaggregation of nonfarm employment indicates that manufacturing employment is growing faster in some nonmetropolitan areas than in metropolitan ones, especially in nondurable goods manufacturing. Despite this greater relative growth, nonfarm jobs are not growing fast enough in rural Texas to offset both the displacement of people from agriculture and the natural population growth in rural areas. If rural incomes are to increase and if outmigration to urban areas is to decline, more and better jobs must be provided in rural areas and the skill levels of rural people must be raised to enable them to meet the requirements of those jobs.

The data suggest the existence of a considerable problem for male employment in rural Texas. While female employment is growing in all areas, male employment is declining everywhere except in East Texas, and it is declining for nonmetropolitan Texas as a whole. The data also reveal a much higher proportion of nonmetropolitan Texas poor families headed by males than for the nation as a whole and relatively high labor force withdrawal and subemployment rates and lower labor force absorption rates for nonmetropolitan males in Texas.

The recommendations suggested by our analysis include the following:

1. *Strengthening and perfecting of manpower programs for rural areas in accordance with the suggestions at the end of Chapter III.*

Past rural development efforts have been handicapped by two related problems. First, rural areas have received a disproportionately small share of public funds and development programs. Second, coordination of the many narrowly defined public programs with the unique needs of the local rural areas has been a problem. Consequently gaps and overlaps have been evident in packages of programs for rural development.

The first problem results partially from the disadvantage of rural areas in competing with larger communities for public funds and programs. Rural areas are unable to get many needed programs because they are unaware of the programs' existence or lack the expertise necessary for application for the programs.

The solution for the second problem requires a field staff with knowledge of the needs and problems of local rural areas, expertise on public programs, and skill in coordinating and expediting programs. Such a field staff, a necessary part of any comprehensive statewide rural development program, would also help remove some of the obstacles rural areas face in acquiring public programs.

Individual coordinators should be incorporated into the federal rural development pilot projects on the project sites. These coordinators should be indigenous to the project area and should receive orientation and training in the aspects of comprehensive rural development programs, which would include economic development, natural resource management, human resource development, and other relevant programs. They should become familiar with the respective public agencies involved. Existing appropriations would be reallocated to cover the costs of this program.

2. *Submission of a proposal for a statewide program of rural development coordinators to the 1975 legislative session.* These coordinators would have the qualifications and training outlined in the first recommendation. Eventually the program would involve from thirty to fifty coordinators covering 150 to 200 rural counties, requiring from $800,000 to $1,500,000 in total funding, with 80 percent from the state and 20 percent from the project areas. These coordinators would cooperate with existing organizations and agencies involved in programs relevant to rural development.

To assure equity of access and reduce manpower planning problems, it is further recommended that the governor limit the geographic area of planning directed by city-oriented mayors who act as sponsors for their SMSAs and surrounding counties. Ancillary manpower planning boards (AMPBs), comprising the "balance of state" in Texas, should conduct manpower planning for all nonmetropolitan areas. Further, the governor should not permit the establishment of single-county AMPBs.

3. *Adoption of allocation formulas for manpower funds that better reflect rural needs.* Rural areas have not received their fair share of federal manpower outlays. Texas should therefore encourage the U.S. Department of Labor to make larger outlays for rural programs and to modify allocation formulas that rely on components such as unemployment rates that imperfectly reflect rural labor market conditions.

Manpower revenue sharing funds funneled through the governor's office to the "balance of state" were allocated for fiscal 1974 according to the U.S. Department of Labor's four-factor system: fiscal 1973 allocation levels, civilian labor force, civilian unemployment, and poverty. A "hold harmless" clause ensured that no planning region (AMPB) received less than 85 percent of fiscal 1973 funding. It is recommended that an additional factor—a measure of underemployment—be added to the allocation formula, since poverty and unemployment do not correctly measure the extent of manpower problems in the "balance of state."

Although no single estimating methodology is satisfactory, perhaps the best estimation of underemployment is that derived by the Economic Research Service of the U.S. Department of Agriculture. This measure relates the "actual" median income of a county to "required" median income, where the required median income is a derived county standard. The derived county standard is the national median income adjusted to reflect the earning capacity of the county labor force if county incomes were the same as those for the national labor force with similar earning characteristics. Statistical series on the following labor force characteristics were used to adjust the national median income:[1]

- Age-race mix (age distribution by white and nonwhite).
- Educational status (attainment).
- Labor force status (income recipient is or is not in the labor force).
- Employment factor (worker is employed, unemployed, or in the armed forces).
- Occupational structure.
- Work experience (length of time spent working in average week).

If either an underemployment index or "subemployment" rate rather than a regular unemployment rate were used in allocation formulas for distributing manpower monies, the result would be to shift larger allocations of funds to rural areas.

Money alone, however, will not solve the problem. Manpower programs should be developed in cooperation with the state to more adequately reflect rural conditions.

4. *Strengthening of manpower delivery capabilities in rural areas.* A major problem for the delivery of manpower services in rural areas is the absence of manpower delivery capabilities. Agents are needed to identify needy individuals and to bring manpower programs to their attention. The manpower coordinators recommended above would be a step in the right direction, but other steps also could be taken. The present experimental Operation Hitchhike program to deliver manpower programs through existing rural agencies like the Extension Service seems promising but is limited by inadequate funds and does not operate in Texas. Many agencies could be identified to carry out rural manpower functions if funds were available.

---

[1]The 1970 estimates of underemployment are currently being made by the U.S. Department of Agriculture. National median income weights for 1970 for age, educational attainment, and work experience groups as well as by labor force, employment, and occupational status are available from the authors or the U.S. Department of Agriculture. For methodology, see U.S. Department of Agriculture, Agricultural Economic Report No. 166.

5. *Coordination of manpower programs with economic development activities.* Careful consideration should be especially given to the "start-up training" concept.

6. *Provision of public employment programs to provide useful work and incomes for the hard-to-employ in rural areas.* Without much faster rates of rural development, many underemployed and unemployed rural Texans, especially men, for whom jobs are apparently declining in many areas, and young people, are not likely to be absorbed in the private sector within reasonable commuting distance of their homes. The Green Thumb program has been relatively successful and should be expanded and combined with Neighborhood Youth Corps programs in accordance with the discussion at the end of Chapter III. Public employment is a relatively efficient and noninflationary way to reduce unemployment.

7. *Careful consideration of the adoption of measures to combat discrimination because of race, sex, and national origin.* Racial and ethnic minorities suffer much more than whites because of inadequate human resource development programs and racial discrimination in employment and the administration of government programs. One third of the population and one half of the poor in rural Texas are members of a minority group.

8. *Extension of unemployment insurance to, and liberalization of workmen's compensation legislation for, agricultural workers.* It also is important to provide adequate enforcement machinery for protective labor legislation in rural areas. We see no convincing arguments for excluding agricultural workers from the benefits of protective legislation. Moreover, these measures would help agricultural employers hold their more experienced and productive workers by overcoming an important competitive disadvantage with nonfarm employers.

9. *Efforts by state officials to ensure that the full potential of the Rural Development Act of 1972 is realized.* State officials should act to make certain that the Rural Development Act of 1972 is fully funded, that the President expends the funds appropriated, and that workable guidelines are adopted. Furthermore, the state should anticipate thoroughly the manpower implications of a wide variety of expected federal legislation.

MANPOWER APPENDIX

DEFINITION OF
MAJOR RURAL MANPOWER PROGRAMS

Following is a brief description of manpower programs listed in Table 26 of the text of this report:

PSC (Public Service Careers):

The Public Service Careers Program has four major plans. Three are designed to meet state and local manpower needs. The fourth is a parallel program in the federal government. The four plans are:

Plan A. Employment and Upgrading in State, County, and Local Governments
Plan B. Employment and Upgrading in Agencies Receiving Federal Grants-in-Aid
Plan C. New Careers in Human Service
Plan D. Employment and Upgrading in the Federal Service

The objective of PSC is to secure, within merit system principles, permanent employment for disadvantaged persons in public agencies at every level, and to stimulate the upgrading of current employees. The PSC program is designed to deal with specific institutional, individual, and environmental barriers that have prevented the employment of the disadvantaged in the public sector. Enrollees are upgraded as they move through a work-training program.

WIN (Work Incentive Program):

Authorized by the 1967 amendments to the Social Security Act, administered by the Department of Labor, WIN provides counseling, assessment, orientation, job development, institutional training, on-the-job training, work experience, and special work projects for members of AFDC families referred by state or local welfare agencies. Child care and other social support services are provided by welfare agencies.

Amendments to the Social Security Act of July 1, 1972, establish stringent national standards for the states to determine which members of the AFDC families must register for work or training to receive full benefits.

CEP (Concerted Employment Program):

Funded to cities and selected rural areas by the U.S. Department of Labor, CEP is a manpower program including many component programs.

NMWP (National Migrant Worker Program):

To make it possible for migrants to leave the migrant stream, the NMWP attempts to provide a comprehensive program of manpower and supportive services to enable the migrant to secure permanent year-round employment that will provide income above the poverty level.

OM (Operation Mainstream):

Offers work opportunities for chronically unemployed adults aged 22 and older—but most participants are 55 or over. It has a rural area emphasis and involves public service employment.

NYC (Neighborhood Youth Corps):

Work-experience and training programs for young people in school (IS) aged 14 and older and out-of-school (OS) youths aged 16-21 authorized by the Economic Opportunity Act. Enrollees may work in the nonprofit or the public sector of the economy and their wages are paid by the federal government.

New Careers (see Plan C of PSC):

New Careers is designed to develop entry-level professional aide jobs in human services areas with maximum career-ladder opportunities.

JOBS (Job Opportunities in the Business Sector):

JOBS involves a concerted effort to place the hardcore unemployed in permanent jobs and is implemented through a variety of training programs involving both government and private industry.

JOPS (JOBS Optional Program):

JOPS offers employers in the private sector the opportunity to hire and train a specified number of disadvantaged and nondisadvantaged persons for permanent employment in jobs that provide an opportunity for advancement. The program also enables employers to upgrade present employees into occupations requiring higher skills. Under a JOP fixed unit cost contract, the contractor receives the extraordinary costs of providing adequate training to individuals hired and trained under the contract. At least 40 percent of these persons must be disadvantaged. JOP is administered by the appropriate state on-the-job training agency (SOJTA) in accordance with the Manpower Development and Training Act of 1962, as amended, and the rules, regulations, policies, and procedures promulgated by the Secretary of Labor pursuant to that act.

Operation SER (Operation Service, Employment, and Redevelopment—and also the Spanish verb "to be"):

Supported by the Department of Health, Education, and Welfare and the Department of Labor. Occupational training and job placement assistance, along with counseling, adult basic education, and English-language instruction, are provided when needed.

OIC (Opportunities Industrialization Center):

OIC is a Philadelphia-based black self-help effort in major cities with emphasis on manpower activities.

Model Cities Manpower and Job Development:

This program's objective is to concentrate the efforts and resources of federal, state, and local public and private efforts to improve the quality of urban life.

The Model Cities Act requires cities to coordinate the efforts of numerous local agencies and institutions in planning, developing, and executing an overall plan for solving the major problems of selected model neighborhoods. Such plans may include construction of housing, health facilities, and schools; expansion of community services; or any other activity designed to improve the quality of life in urban areas, including manpower training and job development.

MDTA Institutional:

Job training, counseling, vocational preparation, basic education, etc., given in job-simulated workshops or in a classroom situation. Administered jointly by the Department of Labor and the Department of Health, Education, and Welfare.

EEA (Emergency Employment Act of 1971):

Gives unemployed and underemployed persons transitional employment in jobs providing needed public services during times of high unemployment and, wherever feasible, related training and manpower services to enable such persons to move into employment or training not supported under this act.

VocEd (Vocational Education):

Educational programs directly related to job training and placement. There are secondary school, postsecondary and adult secondary varieties of VocEd.

Note: The descriptions of manpower programs in this appendix are adapted from the National Association of Counties' *County Manpower Report*, vol. 1 (nos. 1 and 2).

THE SOUTH CAROLINA START-UP TRAINING PROGRAM

Roy Van Cleve*

Start-up industry training received its impetus, in the Southeast, during the 1950s under North Carolina's industrial development program. In the early 1960s South Carolina, using North Carolina's experiences and some of its personnel, started its current program. The North Carolina program is now controlled by the academic community, and there is greater emphasis on the broader educational aspects than in the specific job-oriented industrial training program that South Carolina has successfully maintained.

Virginia also has a start-up program of a slightly different nature, and Alabama began a program modeled after the South Carolina program in 1971. Texas contracted the firm of Harper, Cotton and Little, Inc. (HCL), consultants, who guided the establishment of the Alabama program and previously worked as individuals in both the North and South Carolina programs, to help establish a start-up industry program during 1973, but training program funds were deleted from the budget by the 1973 Texas Legislature. The Texas Education Agency and Texas Industrial Commission, however, have a small start-up training project that apparently will continue despite that deletion.

Twenty-six programs are currently operating or are on the drawing board. South Carolina's program is the current "model" although, according to J. D. Little of HCL, it is now being endangered by the same type of academic emphasis that brought about the deterioration of North Carolina's program.

The success of a start-up industry program is based on simultaneous recruitment, selection, classification, and training of a labor force to meet the specific job requirements of a given firm or industry. There is no wasted motion or effort in training personnel for the labor market in general skills

*Roy Van Cleve is a research associate at the Center for the Study of Human Resources, The University of Texas at Austin.

that may or may not be in demand in the locale in which the worker desires to live. All training is conducted on the basis of specific objectives and jobs to meet known and stated demands in a given locale. The jobs created and the training conducted are of such skill levels, under the program's concepts, that marginal, entry-level jobs paying the minimum wage are leapfrogged and the personnel trained enter the labor force in higher-paying and more demanding positions.

Despite the number of programs in existence and the apparent advantages of start-up training, little documentation is available concerning their implementation and maintenance. Harper, Cotton and Little, recognized industrial development experts, have not documented their efforts because they sell their services in the establishment of a running program. Alabama's program has been in existence for such a short time that it has not been documented, nor has HCL encouraged documentation. In interviews with our staff, South Carolina officials stated that they believed start-up industry training to be one of their sharpest industrial development tools and until recently have had no desire to tell other states, by documenting their efforts, how to build such a tool for fear of losing the competitive edge.

Start-Up in the Black in South Carolina

South Carolina officials contend that the trend in capital investment in the state has been upward since their Technical Education Committee (TEC) initiated its unique system of special schools in 1961. During the period from 1951 to 1961, new plant investment amounted to only $1.4 billion. In the 1962 to 1973 period, new plant investment amounted to $5.9 billion, and in 1973 alone it totaled $1.2 billion. This investment resulted in a continuous increase in South Carolina's corporate taxes.[1]

The dominant factor credited with attracting and locating new industry in the state during this period was the availability of a skilled labor force *trained* to meet industries' specific demands.

The TEC-conducted training is cited by Eichner[2] as an example of what can be done to help new and expanding firms with their labor problems. South Carolina's "systems approach" has nine separate but closely related and interfaced phases. The system is called "Start-Up in the Black in South Carolina," and the Special Schools program is the heart of the system.

---

[1]South Carolina State Committee for Technical Education, *Start-Up in the Black in South Carolina*, brochure, n.d.

[2]Alfred S. Eichner, *State Development Agencies and Employment Expansion*, Policy Papers in Human Resources and Industrial Relations 18, Institute of Labor and Industrial Relations, University of Michigan—Wayne State University, November 1970.

The South Carolina program contains the following phases:

1. *Analysis*. After the initial recruiting effort of South Carolina officials has been completed and a corporation has made the decision to open a new plant in the state, the Division of Industrial Services (DIS) of the TEC visits the corporate headquarters or plants of the firm in their current location. There DIS becomes familiar with the production methods, the precise types of skills that will be needed, and the number of start-up personnel required in each skill category. This analysis of manpower, recruiting, and training needs provides the basis for phase two of the system.

2. *Master Plan*. With the manpower needs specified, a master plan is prepared for recruiting, testing, selecting, and training the workers necessary to meet the firm's demands at the time the new plant is expected to commence operations. The plan, which is then submitted to the firm for approval, contains a complete study of labor availability, skill requirements, wage rates, and fringe benefits for each of the job classifications required.

3. *Lead Time Schedule*. In the process of preparing the master plan a comprehensive lead time schedule is developed. It pinpoints all recruiting, testing, selecting, and training activities. Time is allowed, working backward from the date the plant is expected to open, for the recruitment of the workers, their testing, and the selection and classification of those with different aptitudes. In those cases where aptitude differentiation is required in training, the better prospects are selected for the more demanding training and task performance.

4. *Training Facility Preparation*. Once the plant site selected is announced to the public, the chosen community, where necessary, makes a training facility available to DIS. DIS then equips the facility with the necessary production machinery and instructors to meet the requirements of the lead time schedule. In the event that a TEC center, of which there are thirteen throughout the state, is located in the vicinity of the new plant, its facilities are used in lieu of the community-provided ones. In some cases the facilities at the new plant site are used when the construction has advanced to the point where this is both feasible and desirable. This equipping and staffing is done at no cost to the firm and if any specific machinery or personnel have to be "borrowed" from the firm TEC reimburses the firm for wear and tear or for the time and services of the instructional personnel.

5. *Orientation*. As the training facility is being prepared DIS personnel are conducting orientation for members of the firm who are to be transferred to South Carolina. These orientations cover the mores, customs, housing accommodations, and educational, recreational, and cultural opportunities of the state in general and the chosen community in particular. Officials feel that these orientations have been valuable in easing the doubts and assuring the willingness of key personnel to accept the opportunity for relocation.

Eichner[3] points out that more time and effort is generally devoted to these planning phases and to the detailed planning of the training programs than to their actual implementation. However, the value of these comprehensive and thorough efforts is readily apparent in the successfully executed programs.

6. *Recruiting.* With the initial five phases completed, the actual human resource development begins with the recruitment of a South Carolinian labor force. TEC has compiled lists of under- and unemployed persons in the state as well as a list of all skilled workers in a surrounding seven-state area. These lists are computerized, so that TEC can determine almost immediately the number of potential workers of a given skill level within any given geographic area. The lists indicate that the number of under- and unemployed persons located throughout the state is some three times higher than the official figures. Further, all of the people on these lists are interested enough in better jobs to have completed and returned a TEC questionnaire concerning further technical education. The people on the lists are the primary candidates for the soon-to-be-created jobs, and the lists are the source of recruitment, but the recruiting effort is supplemented by the State Employment Service and by newspaper, radio, and television advertising. TEC tries to obtain at least three fourths of the workers required from an area included in a fifteen-mile commuting radius of the plant. The recruiting is conducted in such a manner that, in accordance with the lead time schedule, the jobs requiring greater skill are the first to be filled.

7. *Selection.* All of the personnel recruited are screened and classified; those persons found most suitable are placed in the training programs. Persons not qualified for the higher skill levels are considered at later dates for jobs requiring less demanding or different skills.

8. *Training.* Those selected for training are expected to attend classes, without compensation and on their own time, five nights a week from 6:30 to 10:00 for six to ten weeks. To ensure the most effective training possible, Analytical Method Training (AMT, a systems approach to training),[4] which teaches the best way of doing a job with the minimum of expenditure of time, motion, and money, is employed. This training, accomplished by the applicants on their own time and without compensation, provides the trainees with an opportunity to look at the firm and vice versa. In South Carolina's experience, the motivated individual trained under these conditions makes the

[3]*Ibid.*, p. 44.

[4]During the research an evaluation of AMT is made by comparing it to the work of Drs. William R. Tracey and C. L. J. Legere in the "Development of Instructional Systems" for the United States Army Security Agency, Training Center and School, Fort Devens, Massachusetts. Dr. Tracey's books *Designing, Training, and Development Systems* and *Evaluating Training and Development Systems* are relied upon extensively in the evaluation.

most reliable employee. Further, it is believed that the motivation engendered in the training is a key factor to the overall success of the Special Schools program.

9. *Job Placement.* Each of the eight phases outlined above is scheduled and interfaced so that in phase nine the trainees are, on an as-required basis, placed on the firm's payroll in such a manner as to ensure that full-scale production operation can commence upon completion of the plant and without any delays due to labor problems.

The program initiated in fiscal 1961-1962 has grown as follows:[5]

Fiscal year	*Trainees*
61-62	475
62-63	2,190
63-64	2,785
64-65	2,824
65-66	5,044
66-67	5,704
67-68	4,081
68-69	4,419
69-70	4,534
70-71	3,804
71-72	5,403
72-73	5,054

The training provided these 46,317 South Carolinians[6] has been given in over 600 Special Schools to meet the exact job requirements of 367 new or expanding industries.

Benefits

In addition to the individual benefits provided (increased job skills), the following benefits have allegedly accrued to South Carolina and all of its citizens during the 1961-1962 to 1971-1972 decade and can be attributed in large part to the Special Schools program.

1. Every county in South Carolina benefited from the industrial growth brought about by Special Schools training.

---

[5]South Carolina State Committee for Technical Education, *TEC in the Seventies, 1970-1971 Progress Report*, brochure, n.d.

[6]South Carolina State Committee for Technical Education, *TEC Notes* 4, no. 44 (November 13, 1972).

2. Additional tax revenues brought about by the increased earnings of South Carolinians and by corporate taxes paid by new and expanding industries resulted in more and better programs for all South Carolinians.

3. More local and state monies for public education were made available in the form of increased salaries for teachers and more modern school buildings.

4. On a per capita basis, South Carolina gathered more investment capital than any other state.

5. The income of South Carolinians grew at a faster rate than the income of residents of any other state.

6. Local and state revenues increased tremendously during the decade of the sixties, with little or no increase in taxes.[7]

Additionally, the DIS or TEC schools have been credited by South Carolina officials with being the primary reasons for the decision of major manufacturers to locate plants in the state. These hundreds of corporations with their thousands of jobs, ranging in size from industrial giants to home-town plants, and manufacturing such diverse products as turbine generators, textured fibers, nuclear fuel assemblies, food processing, high-speed steel taps, and roller bearings, have created a demand in South Carolina for highly skilled, well-paid labor and its supportive services.

Further, South Carolina officials[8] have found this program of such great benefit to the state that they are no longer seeking labor-intensive industries for the Piedmont area and are discouraging such firms from locating in that area. Labor-intensive firms are now being sought and aided only in the Coastal Plains region, considered to be the last underdeveloped region of the state.

Replication of the Program

To date, over forty states and many local governments have formally visited South Carolina, according to state officials, and sought assistance and advice concerning similar programs in their own locales. Since the program has been cited as an example of a progressive way to create job demand and thus assure employment upon the completion of training, replicability of the program is being studied at the Center for the Study of Human Resources, The University of Texas at Austin.

---

[7]South Carolina State Committee for Technical Education, *Guide to Technical Education in South Carolina*, brochure, November 1971.

[8]Woody Brooks, executive director, Division of Local Government, Office of the Governor of South Carolina, interview conducted November 20, 1972.

CONCERTED SERVICES IN TRAINING AND EDUCATION

James L. Webb*

Concerted Services in Training and Education (CSTE) is a small experimental program originally intended to provide better coordination and utilization of existing occupational education programs in small towns and rural areas. There are several unique features in these projects. First, CSTE does not provide new programs or financing but is intended to help participating rural communities by supplying a CSTE coordinator who provides expertise and access to communication. Second, the CSTE program is under the supervision of an interdepartmental task force that includes members from the U.S. Departments of Agriculture, Labor, Health, Education, and Welfare (HEW), Housing and Urban Development (HUD), Commerce, and the Interior; the Office of Economic Opportunity (OEO); the Small Business Administration (SBA); and the regional commissions. Third, the program is funded without new appropriations by some of the participating agencies through their affiliated state agencies—for example, the U.S. Department of Labor sends the funds for the CSTE projects it finances through the state employment services, HEW through state divisions of vocational and technical education.

The CSTE program grew out of a recognition that rural areas had a much higher rate of poverty than urban areas but at the same time had lower average educational attainment and received a proportionately smaller share of federal funds than urban areas. The CSTE approach was conceived to help solve this dilemma in two ways: (1) the CSTE coordinator would provide expertise and assistance that would enable rural communities to compete more successfully with urban areas for federal grants; and (2) CSTE would help existing programs—local as well as federal—to be effective, tailoring them to the functional needs of the community. The primary emphasis was on

---

*James L. Webb is a research associate at the Center for the Study of Human Resources, The University of Texas at Austin.

occupational education programs—vocational education, manpower training, adult basic education.

History and Objectives

The CSTE program grew out of a series of executive orders beginning in 1959.[1] The interdepartmental task force has eighteen members. The cochairpersons are from the U.S. Departments of Labor and Health, Education, and Welfare, and the executive director is from the U.S. Department of Agriculture. The program began with single-county projects in three states in 1966. By 1973 there were twenty-one different projects—some of which were multicounty projects—in fifteen states.[2]

The objectives of the programs were broadly defined but emphasized increasing the employability of rural persons:

1. Development of a means of concentrating available resources on "occupational education problems and as necessary on health, welfare, socioeconomic, and related problems."
2. Identification of existing and potential employment and occupational education opportunities.
3. Making unemployed and underemployed rural persons more employable through improved educational and vocational skills, vocational counseling, and improved health and personal appearance.
4. Demonstration that cooperative occupational education programs, in conjunction with other economic development activities, can significantly increase employment opportunities in rural areas.
5. Demonstration that a cooperative occupational educational effort based on local involvement will develop indigenous leadership and increase individual dignity and community awareness.
6. Determination of the relationship between traditional educational and occupational patterns and present and future needs.

---

[1]Executive Orders 10847, 11122, and 11307. A cabinet-level Rural Development Committee was formed under Executive Order 11122 in May 1964.

[2]The states with CSTE programs were Arkansas, with three projects; Minnesota, New Mexico, and Oklahoma, with two projects each; and West Virginia, Kentucky, Illinois, Montana, Georgia, Nebraska, Texas, Maryland, Maine, South Carolina, and Iowa, with one project each. (Information from executive secretary of Interdepartmental Task Force on Concerted Services in Training and Education in Rural Areas, as of January 1973).

Strategy and Approach

The CSTE strategy for attaining the above objectives involved these measures: (1) legitimation of coordinators with other public officials; (2) coordination of action and instigation of new projects; (3) use of all inputs—local, state, and national; and (4) providing expertise in resource development. The legitimation process was facilitated by choosing a well-known and respected community resident and introducing that person to agency officials through workshops and other means. The CSTE was intended to be flexible while increasing the effectiveness of existing programs with a minimum of expense and disruption of existing agency procedures.

The approach taken by CSTE projects has included three steps: (1) a survey of the project areas' human and economic resources; (2) use of existing occupational education programs and establishment of new training programs under existing statutes; and (3) formulation of policies to develop the community.

A formal evaluation concluded that CSTE has resulted in: (1) community resource surveys; (2) an increase in the size, variety, and course offerings in occupational education programs; (3) increased coordination at the Washington, D.C., level. However, the study did not find any significant expansion of employment opportunities in the project areas studied.[3]

An examination of recent reports of CSTE projects throughout the nation reveals a wide variety of activities. All projects have completed a resource survey including a manpower inventory. At least one coordinator believes this survey has helped attract a manufacturing plant to the project area. Many of the coordinators emphasize economic development either by trying to attract new firms or by encouraging local entrepreneurship. Many new occupational education and adult education programs have been initiated or expanded in areas served by CSTE. The training programs initiated seem to have had widely varying impact on the employability of enrollees. Some have enrolled persons who did not need the training, while others have offered irrelevant courses.

Among activities included are development of community health services, arts and crafts classes, family planning, anti-drug and -alcohol programs, and conservation programs. Probably some of the most effective manpower activities have resulted as side effects of efforts to expand health services and facilities in CSTE communities. Expansion of hospitals or nursing homes has provided employment for low-income workers while simultaneously providing needed services to the communities.

---

[3]B. Eugene Griessman, *Planned Change in Low-Income Rural Areas: An Evaluation of Concerted Services in Training and Education* (Raleigh, North Carolina: North Carolina State University, 1969).

In sum, the activities of CSTE projects are not easily categorized but suggest a tendency to move toward job creation activities while simultaneously promoting diverse community service programs as well as occupational education programs.[4]

CSTE in Red River County, Texas[5]

History and Background

The only CSTE project in Texas is located in the northeast corner of the state, in Red River County. The CSTE program has operated less than two years. The coordinator is a native of the county and a former high school principal in the county.

Red River County has a population of approximately 15,000 persons, 5,000 of whom live in the county seat, Clarksville. Historically the county's economy has been based on cotton growing dating back to the antebellum period. Over the past few years there has been a marked shift to livestock production—primarily raising feeder cattle for sale to feed lots in West Texas and elsewhere. Further, over the last two decades a number of small labor-intensive plants have located in the county.

The net impact of the shift from labor-intensive cotton production to capital-intensive livestock production has not been offset by the inflow of manufacturing jobs. The population declined about 8.6 percent from 1960 to 1970.

The population of Red River County is fairly poor. The median family income was about $4,600 in 1970. Nearly one third (31.3 percent) were below the poverty guideline in 1970, and one fifth of the population received three fourths of poverty level income or less. One person in five in the county is black.[6]

CSTE

The initial undertaking of CSTE in Red River County was a manpower survey. The Smaller Communities Team spent several days instructing area residents and provided some forms, after which the county residents

---

[4]Based on unpublished quarterly narrative reports for all of the CSTE projects for the United States, June 30, 1972, and September 30, 1972.

[5]This section is based on personal interviews with the Red River County CSTE coordinator and other knowledgeable persons in the area in February 1973.

[6]U.S. Bureau of the Census, 1970 Census.

themselves conducted the survey under the coordinator's supervision. Several new training programs have resulted from the coordinator's efforts. A building maintenance course was held at the local vocational school under MDTA. Adult basic education has been expanded, and the coordinator is currently trying to secure some MDTA-JOBS for a local firm. Attempts to secure Operation Mainstream programs have been unsuccessful.

The coordinator, convinced that training programs without available jobs are meaningless, has attempted to expand employment opportunities in the area. He provided expertise in securing an SBA loan for a furniture plant planning to locate in the local industrial park and Farmers' Home Administration loans to improve water and sewer systems in several communities in the county.

However, efforts to attract new manufacturing firms are handicapped by the size of the community. Kohler was considering a plant location there, but the labor force was too small to permit any expansion. Furthermore, the representatives of firms looking for new plant locations often remain anonymous even to the extent of not disclosing the kind of product they produce.

CSTE has helped to establish a community-operated employment service operating two days per week. It has not been very effective, however, because several days usually pass between the listing of a vacancy and the referral of applicants.

The CSTE coordinator has been active in a number of areas that fall into the category of community services, including expansion of health care services and facilities, family planning, an alcoholism rehabilitation program, and numerous other activities.

One of the most important functions of the CSTE is liaison between various agencies. The coordinator is on the boards of the Resource Conservation and Development District and the local industrial foundation and has access to the Council of Government and Economic Development District for the area. In addition, CSTE provides a communication function to citizens and civic organizations and to local governments in nearby counties. The official opposition to social programs has declined significantly in several of these areas, although it would be difficult to pinpoint the cause of this change.

Additional Interviews

Since the CSTE coordinator felt that growth of job opportunities in the area was a key to community development, interviews with plant personnel and tours of several plants were conducted to obtain a rough idea of the effects of past industrialization. All the operations observed were low-wage, labor-intensive operations.

The newest plant in the area is a wholesale book operation that maintains a computerized inventory system of books sold primarily to schools and libraries. About 60 percent of the firm's 175 employees were clerical workers, most of whom keypunched and performed other simple operations in the automated bookkeeping system. These were predominantly young, white females—only three blacks were visible among over fifty employees in the clerical section.

Most of the other employees stack the books on the shelves of the warehouse. Most stackers were white women, but about 15 percent were black.

Another plant assembled doors and windows for mobile homes. Most of the skills required could be acquired in a few days. The work force in this plant was composed predominantly of white males over forty-five years old. The plant manager hired older workers because they were considered far less likely to leave the area. Since this operation has seasonal fluctuations, older workers may also be more willing to work only part of the year.

The third operation visited was the ubiquitous garment factory. However, contrary to the image these factories have in many places, this particular operation has been in the same location for over twenty years. Ninety percent of the employees were women, of whom one third were black.

Most of the other manufacturing operations in the county employ a predominantly male work force whose racial composition varies from nearly all black to mixed to nearly all white. However, all operations had low hourly wage scales—from $1.60 beginning to $2.25 for more skilled workers. Except for the clerical and keypunch work in the book wholesaling firm, few jobs lead to skill upgrading.

Effects on Workers

The existing industrial firms in Red River County and the additional firms the community is likely to attract have not been tied to manpower programs, since only minimal programs have been available. Moreover, manpower training programs do not appear relevant to these firms for several reasons: (1) a surplus of labor supply exists in the county; (2) the skill requirements are low; and (3) the incoming firms are allowed to hire as they please. All three of these conditions appear unlikely to change.

Indications of labor surplus are these circumstances: (1) approximately one fifth of reporting workers commute outside the county, and (2) approximately 300 qualified applicants are on file at the largest firm.

Most of the skills required by the firms are acquired after a few days on the job. For example, according to the aluminum assembly plant manager, most of the jobs in the plant could be learned in two days except for a few aluminum welding jobs requiring several months to learn. The garment workers were hired solely on the basis of manual dexterity and sewing tests.

The book wholesale firm is one of the few that provide some skill upgrading, and this is limited to employees in its data processing operations. Even here, the local labor surplus permits the firm to cream the labor force and to hire mainly high school graduates, although there are some exceptions.

The existing industrial firms are low-wage, low-skill, labor-intensive operations. Prospects for attracting high-wage firms do not seem bright: (1) the labor force is too small to attract large firms, and (2) small high-skill plants generally need ancillary services and a skilled labor force to draw upon—neither of which exists in this small rural county.

Tying subsidies of new firms to commitments to hire disadvantaged workers (with complementary manpower programs where necessary) appears to be an attractive policy but is probably unlikely to be attempted. The principal attraction of rural labor markets is nonunion, low-wage labor. Firms producing labor-intensive goods in highly competitive markets that are trying to avoid unions are not likely to accept restrictions on hiring practices by other groups either, and some community probably will always offer subsidies without restrictions.

In short, attraction of labor-intensive manufacturing can absorb and has absorbed some of the labor displaced from agriculture, including some disadvantaged workers, but it is not likely to provide much upgrading, especially for minority members.

Relation of CSTE to Local Government

The county judge, Gavin Watson, considered the CSTE program quite valuable to the community because "the federal government doesn't give you anything—you have to take it," that is, considerable expertise is required to acquire federal grants. The judge also pointed out that the CSTE coordinator helps fill the leadership vacuum in rural areas. For example, in Red River County—as in most other rural counties—the commissioners are "road commissioners" and have little interest in providing anything beyond roads and bridges. Moreover, an institution that formerly provided some community cohesion in many areas—the local school district—is gone because of consolidation. The CSTE coordinator helps to fill this void while at the same time increasing community awareness of the need for increased community social services and community development. The leadership void is reflected in

Judge Watson's story of a mayor in Red River County who had received a revenue sharing check and wanted to send it back because he was reluctant to do the paper work.

Though the county judge believed that CSTE was quite valuable to the community, he thought it quite unlikely that the county would assume the cost of CSTE if it were not federally funded, even with revenue sharing funds, because most of the revenue sharing money will go toward bringing the county jail and solid waste disposal system into compliance with judicial and federal guidelines.

The shift to revenue sharing may change the nature and effectiveness of the CSTE approach. If revenue sharing funds are funneled through governors, mayors, and county judges with essentially no strings attached, the need for the CSTE coordinator's "grantsmanship" abilities should decrease. With revenue sharing, these same mayors, county judges, and governors might be less disposed toward the relative emphasis of human resource programs in CSTE.

Assuming that some categorical programs for rural areas remain, there is a question of the replicability of the CSTE approach. In the period before revenue sharing, the CSTE coordinator could be an effective "grantsman" because of familiarity with the guidelines, application procedures, the members of Washington, D.C., agencies, and the local decentralized federal entities such as the Rural Conservation and Development Committees (RC&Ds) and Economic Development Districts (EDDs).

Prior to revenue sharing, replication of the CSTE program's effectiveness in grantsmanship seemed difficult after the program reached a certain size. There are more than 2,000 rural counties that probably require at least 700 coordinators. Several additional layers of bureaucracy would probably be required between the coordinators and Washington.

On the other hand, decentralization of federal programs by giving regional offices of federal agencies more authority would permit the CSTE approach to be effective, but emphasis would be placed on liaison with regional, rather than Washington, D.C., offices of federal agencies. Thus, the personal contact could probably be maintained between the coordinators and the regional agencies without intervening levels of administrative machinery.

Revenue sharing as envisioned under P.L. 92-512, however, is not decentralization of federal programs but defederalization of control of federal funds given to other levels of government. In the case of revenue sharing, the CSTE coordinator would be one among many program administrators going to mayors, county judges, and governors. The coordinator would have little political or financial leverage and is likely to have influence only through his expertise, which is limited at present by lack of staff.

An apparent weakness of CSTE as it has operated in the past is the absence of a coherent strategy for rural development, once the initial labor and resource surveys are made. However, the lack of a coherent development strategy probably results largely from the conceptualization of the program rather than from individual failings of coordinators. Specifically, CSTE was undertaken in the belief that by improving rural labor forces through implementation and coordination of occupational education programs, both rural areas and their residents could be developed, assuming that other rural development programs would also be present. Often other rural development programs are not present in rural areas. The coordinator is left to wrestle with the dilemma of whether to promote occupational education (and hope this will induce economic growth), to devote attention mainly to economic development (so that future trainees will have jobs in the community), or to find some compromise approach.

Evaluation of CSTE

An attempt could be made to evaluate CSTE in terms of its objectives. However, this is quite difficult to do systematically since (1) CSTE has multiple and broad objectives; (2) the CSTE coordinator is supposed to act as a catalyst—initiating, promoting, and expediting but not following up once a project is safely under way; and (3) the CSTE coordinators are encouraged by the task force to maintain "a low profile"—i.e., not to take credit for their help to projects lest some of the cooperating agencies be offended.

On this basis, evaluation of the CSTE program is almost impossible, since it contains several potentially conflicting objectives. For example, in order to increase the acceptance of the coordinator among participating agencies coordinators are encouraged to take no credit for the program's achievements, but the building of community awareness might require some publicity. A fundamental constraint is that the individual CSTE project consists of one person—the coordinator—who has full responsibility for developing the training and programs along with complementary programs to deal with "health, welfare, socioeconomic, and related problems" and to encourage the development of indigenous leadership, individual dignity, and community awareness. Since the coordinator is selected from the community, it is not always possible to hire an expert in manpower training or rural economic development. In most cases the coordinators consequently have not concentrated on occupational education but have spread their efforts among many diverse and unrelated projects. Judging from a remark of one of the task force's cochairpersons, CSTE was intended to concentrate on increasing the employability of residents in the CSTE project areas.[7] In this sense, the CSTE program has not been overwhelmingly successful. Some of the training programs initiated were of dubious value in increasing employability—partially because of the scarcity of job opportunities in the project areas. Because of this scarcity and also because coordinators tend to identify strongly with the project community, there has been a relative shift from the original "people-building" emphasis to a "place-building" (or perhaps, more accurately, place-maintaining) emphasis.

The CSTE program has probably been worth much more to Red River County and to the other project areas than it has cost—for example, the Red River CSTE costs $22,000 per year, while the average annual figure quoted by the executive director of the task force is $30,000 per project. However, the impact of CSTE on increasing employability of residents through training and educational programs appears less substantial.

Rather than an orthodox benefit-cost appraisal of CSTE—which is practically impossible in view of the poorly specified objectives and functions and the unquantified and unquantifiable activities of the coordinators—a "search evaluation"[8] seems more appropriate.

The CSTE program, like other rural development programs, has tended to become involved in many activities outside its original sphere of action. A study of rural development programs by the Brookings Institution[9] suggests that all federal-local programs require coordinating agencies which need to perform certain functions in order to make the programs effective: (1) provide simple and reliable information flows between local communities and federal agencies; (2) promote new programs; (3) furnish technical assistance in preparing proposals, grant applications, etc.; (4) design a development strategy—i.e., set investment priorities; (5) mobilize resources—including overcoming defeatism in the community; (6) coordinate interdependent projects; and (7) expedite ongoing projects—e.g., by interpretation of guidelines.

In terms of search evaluation, CSTE has performed, with varying degrees of proficiency, the functions of a coordinating agency for rural development except for the design of a development strategy. This shortcoming can be explained by several factors: (1) CSTE has no power to enforce any

---

[7]John S. McCauley, "Manpower Developments in Rural Areas," *Employment Service Review* (March-April 1968).

[8]See Glen C. Cain and R. G. Hollister, "Evaluating Manpower Programs for the Disadvantaged," *Cost-Benefit Analysis of Manpower Policies*, edited by G. G. Sommers and W. D. Wood, for an explanation of the problems of evaluating programs with vague and multiple objectives.

[9]James L. Sundquist and David W. Davis, *Making Federalism Work: A Study of Program Coordination at the Community Level* (Washington, D.C.: Brookings Institution, 1969).

development strategy; (2) the coordinators generally lack expertise in the formulation of development strategy; (3) the geographic unit where the CSTE project operates may contain no viable growth point; and (4) specification of an explicit development strategy would make conflicts between "place-oriented" goals and "people-oriented" (especially low-income people) goals apparent.

Conclusions and Recommendations

The CSTE program has been beneficial to the project areas, helping them to obtain new federal programs and introducing the concept of human resource development to rural leadership. Although CSTE has been instrumental in bringing new programs into rural communities and expanding old programs, the human resource development programs have not been successfully tied to job development. The program has been low in cost—approximately $30,000 per project—and worth this amount in the services provided to the rural communities.

In several ways, however, the CSTE concept of encouraging indigenous initiative could be improved. First, as long as ultimate rural development goals remain ambiguous, a coherent and effective rural development program is unlikely. Specifically, there are likely to be fundamental conflicts between the goal of "saving a place"—i.e., reversing population decline, increasing retail sales—and the goal of providing more opportunities for rural residents. If these conflicts remain unreconciled and largely unrecognized, it seems unlikely that CSTE will be effective either in "saving a place" or in "saving the people" in the place.

Second, most of the CSTE coordinators seem to have been aware of the need to tie human resource development programs to the development of new job opportunities, but they lack the resources and expertise necessary for this formidable task. CSTE has helped rural communities to get more piecemeal programs but has not resulted in a coordinated human resource and economic development program.

Third, even if the CSTE coordinators remain as "grantsmen"—rather than assuming the more ambitious role enunciated by the task force—they need a more sophisticated understanding of rural economic and human resource development problems.

Recognizing that the uncertainties brought by the current changes in the structure of intergovernmental relations make any recommendations hazardous, the following recommendations are made:

1. The actions of coordinators of CSTE (or of any agency with a similar role) should be based on a coherent and internally consistent rural

development strategy. This implies that the situation in rural areas must be systematically analyzed, that the objectives of rural development must be specified in operational terms, and that strategies developed must recognize both the constraints discovered in the analysis and the conflicts among the objectives.

2. If a CSTE-type agency is to pursue the broad objectives outlined by the task force, a multicounty project area is recommended, because this would permit the hiring of some professional staff. The multicounty areas would be more likely to contain viable growth points and would have more political leverage than single-county units.

3. The original CSTE objectives outlined by the task force emphasized occupational education as the key to rural development. The flexibility of the CSTE program has allowed the emphasis of operating CSTE projects to shift to job development and provision of services to their rural communities. There seem to be two models of lagging rural areas: (a) areas with relatively high percentages of children and elderly persons but with a fairly well-paid labor force, although these areas may have been experiencing high outmigration due to shifts in demand for products produced in the area, depletion of natural resource inputs, or increased use of labor-displacing technology; and (b) economically stagnant areas that have low wages, high rates of underemployment and unemployment, and excess labor supply.

Elements of both these models are found in most lagging rural areas, but, for example, rural areas in the Great Plains resemble the first model while parts of South Texas resemble the second model more closely. These two models are significant because they imply different strategies for rural development. The implicit development strategy of CSTE has been to improve labor supply in rural areas via occupational education programs while simultaneously increasing labor demand in the local private sector via promotion of economic development. This strategy is more consistent with the second model—provided that economic development is feasible in the area—and should yield benefits both to the "place" as well as to some low-income workers. In the first model, however, the poverty problem is outside the labor force, suggesting a strategy of supplying needed services—especially health services (such as nursing home care) and educational services—which would create an increased demand for labor in the public sector. Much of the additional labor required would be unskilled. There would be a need for some semiskilled and skilled labor, however, and some training programs might be required. In fact, all lagging areas are likely to have substantial portions of disadvantaged persons too young or too old to be in the labor force. Therefore, it is recommended (a) that a "public service-public employment" strategy be given explicit consideration where appropriate; and (b) that the currently favored CSTE strategy of "occupational education-private sector development" not be allowed to supplant the original CSTE objective of improving the opportunities available to rural residents, although this is important in areas that are not viable for economic development.

4. The above recommendations suggest that a CSTE program by itself is not sufficient to develop and implement an effective strategy for rural development. Therefore it is recommended (a) that states develop statewide development strategies consistent with *needs* and *resources* of rural areas; and (b) that states designate several multicounty rural development districts covering the entire state.

5. The CSTE coordinators should develop more expertise in human resource development and rural economic development theory and problems. This recommendation is justified with or without the implementation of other recommendations.

6. The CSTE approach to trying to legitimize the role of the coordinator is desirable and should be retained. Having multicounty projects rather than single-county projects makes this legitimation process more difficult, but the advantages of multicounty project areas outweigh this difficulty if CSTE is to have a true coordinating function.

7. The CSTE program should be retained in its present form if the only alternative is discontinuation of the program.

8. Even in its present form and without implementation of the other recommendations above, CSTE should be expanded substantially. However, the expansion of CSTE past some critical maximum will probably run into diminishing returns, assuming that "grantsmanship" is approximately a zero-sum game.

OPERATION MAINSTREAM IN TEXAS

James L. Webb*

Green Thumb[1]

A review of the Texas Green Thumb program may provide a better understanding of the nature and limitations of Operation Mainstream (OM). Green Thumb in Texas provides work and income for poor, older, male rural residents. The program focuses mainly on income maintenance—80 percent of state Green Thumb funds is spent for wages and fringe benefits for the enrollees—and little is provided for training, supportive services, or placement. The enrollees usually work in racially integrated crews of seven on physical improvement projects for public and private nonprofit agencies, which supply the necessary materials and equipment.

Administratively, the state director of Green Thumb is part of the state Farmers Union office in Waco. There are two field supervisors, one for eight Panhandle-South Plains counties and one for five Central Texas counties.

Since there are many more potential Green Thumb enrollees in Texas than positions available, the program's administrators divide full-time positions among enrollees. For instance, in January 1972, 209 enrollees shared 172 full-time slots. All of the enrollees were over fifty-five years of age, and 127 were over sixty-five; there were fifty-five blacks, thirty-seven Mexican Americans, one Indian, and three women enrolled. Average annual pre-enrollment income was $1,100.

There was no systematic selection process for enrollees. Slots ordinarily were filled from among qualified applicants on a first-come, first-served basis. Crew foremen sometimes solicited applicants, but applicants usually heard of the program by word of mouth and through other informal channels.

---

*James L. Webb is a research associate at the Center for the Study of Human Resources, The University of Texas at Austin.

[1]This section is based on interviews with Texas Green Thumb enrollees and staff. Data are from the state Green Thumb office in Waco.

Apparently little effort was made to verify the statements on applications. Although no systematic effort is made to select hard-core unemployed, personal observations lead to the conclusion that most of the Green Thumb enrollees probably could not find employment elsewhere. There were, for example, two mental patients on one crew. Many of the crew members were in their seventies, and several had slight disabilities.

Although most enrollees are disadvantaged, there was an element of creaming in the Texas program. The crew foremen generally were younger and more skilled than other crew members. Some crew foremen could have found other employment, although it is doubtful that the crews could have functioned without them. Ability to speak English appeared to be an informal requirement, and since the crews often were employed some distance from their homes, some potential participants probably were excluded by lack of transportation. Creaming also sometimes resulted from the use of program positions for political patronage.

The projects involved brush cutting, cleaning up, painting, concrete work, stone laying (for walls), making picnic benches, and building playground equipment. Host agencies included park departments, a church, a Boy Scout camp, juvenile detention centers, county commissioners, and a girls' home. Thus the only kind of instruction (beyond safety training) was informal on-the-job training for minimal to moderate skill levels. Most of the projects involved building new facilities or improving old ones. Generally these facilities were not in poor neighborhoods. However, some of the work might have violated the maintenance of effort clause—e.g., routine maintenance of county property. The Green Thumb staff sought to avoid projects of the brush-cutting type, which create a poor image in host communities. However, routine maintenance work sometimes was accepted to appease host agencies and to provide work for enrollees.

The program had two apparent goals: (1) provision of income for aged men through employment on projects of social benefit and (2) program expansion. The second goal seems to have influenced the choice of activities, with a strong preference for highly visible permanent construction programs. Moreover, publicity—the use of distinctive uniforms for Green Thumb enrollees, news story releases, dedication ceremonies—was consciously used to promote public support for Green Thumb.

Little was done to improve the employability of Green Thumb enrollees, and there was little turnover on the crews in the first two years of the program's operation in Central Texas. The small amount of turnover was due to health or personal reasons, not to employment elsewhere. Moreover, there seemed to be little relationship between the Green Thumb project and public agencies capable of rendering supportive services to Green Thumb participants.

In short, the Green Thumb project has effectively improved the incomes of a number of poor older workers, but, other than the significant improvement in the mental attitudes of the enrollees, the needs of the enrollees—needs for supportive services, training, and placement—were largely ignored.

Overview of Regional OM Programs[2]

The regionally contracted OM programs represent over two thirds of the total OM enrollment. These programs differ in three major respects from their national counterparts: administrative arrangement, characteristics of enrollees, and program goals. In the regional programs, the selection of local program sponsors is the responsibility of the regional manpower administrators (RMAs). Although the RMAs may in practice add to or modify program guidelines, the DOL merely monitors and does not supervise actual OM operations. The national eligibility guidelines are a minimum age of twenty-two, family income below the poverty level, and chronic unemployment or underemployment. At least 40 percent of the enrollees must be over fifty-five years old.

There are two main types of regional programs: (1) projects that are part of Concentrated Employment Programs (CEPs) and (2) programs under the Economic Opportunity Act (EOA). The CEP programs had 2,052 OM enrollees in forty-two local projects in 1971. Most of these programs were in urban areas. The EOA programs had 8,490 enrollees in 310 primarily rural local programs in 1971.

The characteristics of enrollees vary considerably between individual programs, but in general the regional programs have younger enrollees; the mean age is about forty-one or forty-two. The CEP OM programs have mostly blacks, while the other regional programs have a majority of white enrollees. A national evaluation of CEP OM found the average age lower, incidence of possible guideline violations higher, and amount of training received somewhat less than in the EOA programs.[3]

In contrast to the nationally contracted programs, the regional programs emphasize permanent placement in competitive employment as a primary goal and are not as concerned about community services. Regional program

[2]This section is based on Dale W. Berry, Nancy Sandusky, Steven van Dresser, and Joanne Fink, *National Evaluation of Operation Mainstream, Phase III: Regionally Administered Programs* (Washington, D.C.: Kirschner Associates, August 1971); Dale W. Berry, Nancy Sandusky, Steven van Dresser, and Joanne Fink, *National Evaluation of Operation Mainstream, Phase III: Regionally Administered Programs (Supplemental Report)* (Washington, D.C.: Kirschner Associates, October 1971).

[3]Berry, *et al., Phase III*, p. 15.

emphasis tends to cause the selection of younger, more employable applicants, the selection of work stations on the basis of training and placement opportunities rather than of potential community service, and the imposition of time limitations on enrollment (usually three months to two years).

Regional OM Programs in Central and South Texas[4]

The four regionally contracted OM programs studied in Central and South Texas may not be typical of other areas, but their experience illustrates some of the strengths and weaknesses inherent in the regional OM programs.

The RMA monitors these OM programs in New Braunfels, Laredo, Rio Grande City, and Brownsville, with 132, 132, 49, and 138 slots, respectively. The local contractors are all private nonprofit corporations that are part of, or closely related to, community action agencies (CAAs). These programs have a high degree of operational autonomy; DOL monitoring seeks primarily to ensure compliance with eligibility guidelines and to encourage high placement-to-enrollment ratios. Each program is funded at $3,800 per slot.

Surprisingly, none of the program directors or field coordinators interviewed felt that the large geographic areas served presented a problem, although the program director covering the largest area felt that geographic dispersion was a disadvantage in the Neighborhood Youth Corps program, for which his agency also had responsibility. Seemingly, the main difference was that the large area covered by OM programs afforded more potential work stations for enrollees, while geographic distances presented problems for Neighborhood Youth Corps enrollees, who had less access to transportation.

The quality of training in the OM programs depended a great deal on the type of work station the enrollees received, since all vocational training, except that of licensed vocational nurses (LVNs), was accomplished on the job.

The law requires work stations to be in public or private nonprofit organizations. These stations tend to be either "one-on-one" or "crew" projects. Under the one-on-one arrangement, a supervisory or experienced worker in the host agency typically serves as instructor. An enrollee might, for example, be assigned to a water treatment plant to help the operator and to acquire the skills necessary to become licensed.

The crew work stations involve a group of enrollees working on one project under the supervision of host agency personnel, OM staff, or a combination of the two. The amount of training provided can vary

[4]This section is based primarily on interviews with district Manpower Administration staff, directors and staff of individual contractors, and data collected from the files of those contractors.

considerably. Some of the crew assignments merely involve routine maintenance and clean-up work. Others involve jobs that do more to develop skills: heavy equipment work, carpentry, bricklaying, and painting.

In two of the programs, a number of enrollees take LVN training subcontracted to local hospitals. Prior to entering the LVN program the enrollees are given full-time classroom training to enable those without a high school diploma to get a general equivalency diploma and prepare them for the institutional nurse's training.

Use of on-the-job training in work stations has both advantages and disadvantages. The OM program is dependent on the goodwill of the host agency for work with good training possibilities—e.g., whether a road maintenance crew uses front-loaders and bulldozers or shovels and axes depends on the attitude of the county commissioners. Further, usually only a few of the enrollees can expect to be hired by the host agency.

The use of project work stations illustrates some basic contradictions in the OM legislation. Operation Mainstream work can be quite useful to the community—a firehouse, two school cafeterias, and other public facilities were built by projects studied—but the one-on-one work stations, while generally not expanding or improving community services, usually offer training in more marketable skills to the host agency or other employers. The crew work station offers a compromise, permitting younger, more adaptable workers to acquire new skills while older workers, with less potential, work together under a single supervisor. Host agencies do hire enrollees, but since projects usually involve large amounts of labor for short durations, only a few enrollees can expect to be hired by the host agency. Nevertheless, the directors of the regional OM programs in Texas devote considerable attention to job development and often succeed in getting host agencies to hire enrollees, even when this necessitates waiving normal hiring qualifications.

The younger participants tend to receive more classroom instruction, while older workers usually do little more than learn to write their names. The average amount of classroom instruction is somewhat less than a day a week. In some programs, enrollees are required to attend one day a week of basic education, while in other programs the amount of classroom instruction varies according to the vocational needs and capabilities of the enrollees. In the EOA program, where feasible, enrollees were prepared to pass the general equivalency diploma examination.

The OM legislation requires maintenance of effort from host agencies—i.e., OM enrollees cannot be used to do work that would have been done without them, and enrollees are not to displace employed workers. Moreover, the work done by OM enrollees is supposed to provide new or expanded services to the community. That the OM experience is mixed in Texas is not surprising, in view of the conflict between the goals of placement and community service. It is difficult to determine whether OM completers get jobs that would have gone to nonparticipants. Of course, some of the enrollees acquire skills in short supply. A prime example of this is the LVN enrollee, many of whom have remained in rural communities where medical service is sorely needed.

The OM programs render community services by expanding public facilities and public services. Examples of the former in the programs studied were recreational facilities, a new firehouse, two new school cafeterias, an old house refurnished and converted into a museum, and improvement of country roads by installation of cattle guards. In one Texas city, OM participants renovated substandard housing for poor people. In this case, paint and materials were furnished by a civic club. OM participants render service as clerical aides, teachers' aides, and day care assistants.

A national evaluation of Operation Mainstream has criticized the regional programs for violating Congressional intent by minimizing income maintenance. Obviously a program with a time limit on enrollment cannot be a permanent income maintenance program, but even temporary enrollment in OM can permanently improve income for older workers since they receive quarters of social security credit. This can be quite important for older agricultural workers who lack enough quarters of eligibility to receive social security benefits. In fact, in the selection of enrollees one rural OM program gave weight to whether enrollment would make older workers eligible for social security benefits.

The legislative intent was for Operation Mainstream to help remove institutional barriers to the employment of disadvantaged workers, especially older workers. The primacy of the placement goal among the regional programs makes relations with local governments crucial because of their role as potential hosts or employers of terminees. One local OM program director cited the downplaying of OM-CAA relations (the OM program was moved out of the building housing the CAA) as one of the reasons why the OM program was now successful. This particular CAA had incurred the wrath of local government officials, making it difficult to place OM graduates. In this case, local officials lowered the educational requirement in order to hire OM enrollees.

In three of the four programs studied, the data file on enrollees was incomplete and inaccurate. Particularly lacking were follow-up data. The one OM program that itself certified eligibility in general kept good records, including follow-ups, but did not consistently record ethnic characteristics of enrollees. Of the four programs studied, this was the only one where ethnic data were important, since Mexican Americans predominated in the others.

Information on one Texas regional Operation Mainstream program, including some statistics on enrollment and placement rates, is fairly complete.

This program probably is not typical in that it has been more successful than most with job placements. This program is sponsored by the Community Council of South Central Texas (CCSCT) at New Braunfels, which started October 20, 1967. This program served twenty-seven Central Texas counties with a population of 295,000; of these, 40,000 persons were classified as poor. As of April 15, 1971, this program, with an annual enrollee quota of 132, had served 770 enrollees, 140 of whom were currently enrolled and 630 of whom had been terminated. Of those who had been terminated, 419 (66.5 percent) were placed in jobs; only twenty-eight who had completed the program were not initially placed. Follow-up studies indicate that after six months, 90 percent were still employed in the jobs in which they were placed. Only five people had dropped out of the program, and the others were terminated for a variety of personal reasons; only nineteen (3 percent) were terminated for "lack of progress"; ten went on social security; and eight became ineligible.

The ages of enrollees in the CCSCT program were:

22-34	247
35-44	148
45-54	94
55-64	249
65 or older	32

These enrollees clearly were much younger than Texas Green Thumb participants.

Of the 770 total enrollees, ninety-five were on welfare; 541 were heads of households; fifty-one were physically handicapped; only three had incomes above the poverty level; 402 were males; 368 were females; approximately 55 percent were Mexican American; 35 percent were Anglo; and 70 percent had no high school at all. Program costs were $1,780 per enrollee, $2,550 per termination, and $4,000 per placement.

Despite data problems and distortions to create success stories, the Texas regional OM programs seem to have been reasonably successful in achieving employment upgrading for enrollees—particularly in view of the low average skill and education levels. All of the local programs placed at least one fifth of their terminees. Others, such as the LVN trainee program, found jobs for all who completed the training, presumably without displacing any existing workers.

If the "de facto mission" of manpower policy is considered to be to increase the employability of disadvantaged persons, the regional OM programs in Texas are doing quite well, considering the handicaps they face. Although a national evaluation has criticized the regional programs because they failed to follow the original intent of the legislation, the fault seems to lie as much with the legislation, since it enumerates a number of conflicting objectives besides placement. Moreover, since Operation Mainstream is the only manpower program in many rural areas, it is not surprising that directors are under pressure not to limit their programs to older workers.

Funding is inadequate for a program with high priority on placement. The programs receive $3,800 per slot annually. If the enrollees received $1.60 per hour (the minimum under federal law) and worked forty hours per week and fifty weeks a year, there would remain $600 per enrollee per year for fringe benefits, training costs, supportive services, administrative costs, job development, follow-up, data collection, and all the other features necessary for an efficient program.

The regional OM programs also face problems in trying to serve both older and younger workers. The older workers are difficult to place and are less receptive to training. The administrators of the local projects would prefer not to have to enroll a minimum number of older workers, who lower placement averages, the primary criteria used by the DOL in evaluating these programs.

The third major problem for the regional programs is depressed economic conditions of rural areas, which limit the number of available work slots and placement opportunities after enrollment.

The regional OM programs studied were able to help most of their participants. Presumably, all enrollees benefited financially from the temporary income maintenance received during enrollment. Some workers' skills were upgraded, and some workers were permanently placed in unsubsidized employment. The program is low in cost because of the on-the-job training used—whether in the "one-on-one" or "crew" work stations. Although data for even rough measurement are not available, from a social point of view the benefits probably far outweigh the costs, since over 80 percent of the $4,103 cost per "man-year" is for wages and fringe benefits to enrollees, a transfer presumably desired by society. The benefits of expanded community facilities and services undoubtedly exceed the nonwage portion of the cost. Moreover, since OM is often the only manpower or public employment program available to disadvantaged rural adults, it obviously is the "best" program available, and it is better for the participants and for society than a complete reliance on welfare.

PROBLEMS OF MIGRANTS AND MEXICAN AMERICANS

Ray Marshall, R. Lynn Rittenoure, and James L. Walker

Migrant Programs

Of a number of programs adopted to help migrants, one of the earliest was the Annual Worker Plan (AWP) started in 1954. This plan was designed to coordinate the demand and supply for migrant labor, thereby reducing the time between jobs. The employment service agencies in supply states, mainly Texas and Florida, determine the numbers of migrants available, and the agencies in the demand states determine the amount of labor needed. From this information, an agricultural worker schedule is prepared as an itinerary for a migratory crew or family. The number of groups using the AWP has declined since 1967-1969, however, primarily because of mechanization and changing production techniques.[1] According to the Texas Good Neighbor Commission's 1970 annual report, the AWP also has been in trouble since 1967 because employers who were not in compliance with the new housing regulations were not allowed to use the plan.

> The failure of many employers to comply with the new (housing) standards has almost blown the Plan out of the window. . . . the decreases are slowing somewhat but that is of little solace when we survey the damage already done to our system of job placement; the mutual commitment is badly weakened.[2]

Another project designed to test new methods for dealing with migrant problems was the Manpower Administration's migrant demonstration project started in ten states in 1969. The purpose of this project was to "explore ways to help migrants either leave the migrant stream or, if they wanted to

---

[1]"The Annual Worker Plan in 1970," *Rural Manpower Developments* (September-October 1971), p. 26.

[2]Good Neighbor Commission, *Texas Migrant Labor*, annual report (1970), p. 3 of summary.

remain in it, to get any supportive assistance they needed."[3] The project made it possible for local employment offices to hire persons with the job title of "rural outreach interviewer" (ROI) to work with migrants. This approach was in keeping with the U.S. Department of Labor's attempt to change its rural manpower approach so that, instead of merely supplying labor to employers, it would be more responsive to the needs of workers. The plan called for testing various ways to help migrants through a demonstration project involving 750 families selected in Texas by ROIs. This plan was abandoned, however, because many of the migrants could not be located in the stream and other families were selected in order to carry out the project.

Because of defects in the project design and the absence of a careful evaluation, it is difficult to know what effect the migrant demonstration project had. The best feature of the project apparently was the use of ROIs as bridges between local employment offices and migrants.

> The ROI's played a key role in the project and needed dedication and a broad background. They had to be sensitive to migrant views, know local resources, be able to deal skillfully with a variety of agencies, be willing to work odd and long hours, and be able to exert pressure in meeting migrant needs.[4]

The ROIs were particularly useful in helping migrants find housing, health facilities, and jobs, in providing much other assistance to workers making the transition from the migrant stream, or in improving their conditions in it. They apparently accomplished a great deal in making manpower, welfare, and education agencies more responsive to the migrants' needs. After two years, however, the program was discontinued, and the states were supposed to build services to migrants into their regular procedures.[5]

Although statistics are not available, there is agreement that the project did not settle many migrants out of the stream. Apparently the project encountered a number of obstacles including considerable variation in effectiveness of the ROIs; the selection of too large and unwieldy a sample at the outset; the reluctance of consumer states to build services to settle out migrants, whom many considered to be undesirable "outsiders"; and basic defects in selecting goals that were too broad and not carefully selecting target areas for the migrants. A basic problem seems to have been that the employment services and other agencies in labor-consumer states were not interested in rendering services to "Texas Mexicans." A Texas authority, who wishes to remain anonymous, reported, after the first year, "In effect, all we

---

[3]Patricia Marshall, "From Migrant Stream to Mainstream," *Manpower* (July 1971), p. 11.

[4]*Ibid.*, p. 12.

[5]Cora S. Cronemeyer, "New Ways of Helping Migrants," *Rural Manpower* (March 1972), p. 19.

have really learned from this project is that the migrants' problems and difficulties are virtually the same as we have known them to be for years, and that attempting to obtain coordination and cooperation on a large, interstate scale is infinitely more complex than was originally presumed."

National Migrant Worker Plan

In 1971 the U.S. Department of Labor announced a new program, the National Migrant Worker Plan (NMWP), to help workers make the transition from migrant agriculture to stable nonagricultural employment. The NMWP program grew out of the migrant experiment and demonstration (E&D) project and was designed to settle out 5,800 migrants the first year. The program's main strategy is to provide training and job development in the home base area and programs to settle people out of the migrant stream. Mobility facilitation units coordinate services from central locations along the migratory stream. The manpower specialists attached to these units will be able to provide job development, basic education, occupational counseling, supplementary training, and financial assistance. Other agencies also will provide services of various kinds.

The Labor Department has enumerated specific objectives important to the accomplishment of the NMWP's primary goal:

1. provision of comprehensive delivery of services through the most effective combination of service agencies and organizations,
2. redirection of traditional state Employment Service (ES) activities toward needs of migrant workers,
3. increased participation of migrants in development and operation of programs,
4. creation of "the greatest amount of flexibility . . . to deal effectively with the unique . . . problems [of] the migrant work force,"
5. increasing employability of migrants through training and supportive services, and
6. elimination of discriminatory practices that affect migrants because they are mobile and largely ethnic or racial minorities.

In terms of broad strategy, NMWP distinguishes between the programs provided in the home base areas and in demand states. The greater economic opportunities in demand areas imply that outreach, training, and a high level of supportive services are necessary for a successful resettlement of migrants. The economic stagnation of migrants' home base areas requires a more diverse approach, including training, employment, and supportive services that would enable some migrants to relocate from the home base areas, others to enter private employment, and others to enter public employment. Emphasis is placed on public employment since prospects in the private sector are limited in some home base areas and relocation is difficult and expensive.

There is no set mix of components in an individual program. Although sponsors of NMWP projects are encouraged to coordinate the resources of existing agencies into a comprehensive program for migrants, a broad range of components may receive NMWP funding: (1) outreach and recruiting; (2) certification of eligibility, intake, vocational testing and orientation, provision of employability development teams, counseling, and basic education; (3) training; (4) relocation services, job development, and employment; (5) supportive services and placement; and (6) follow-up.

The certification of eligibility is to be undertaken by the local employment service. A problem may develop here since a suggested criterion for certification of a prospective enrollee (as a bona fide migrant) is participation in the Annual Worker Program in the previous year. This guideline would probably exclude the majority of migrants from participation in the NMWP, since most migrant workers do not use the Annual Worker Plan. However, some test will probably be necessary if NMWP is to serve only migrants. This is especially true of home base areas.

Among training programs, institutional training is expected to be a "significant" part. Many migrants have less than the minimum level of education necessary to benefit from institutional training. For example, it has been the informal policy of the Texas Employment Commission not to accept enrollees for MDTA institutional training unless they can perform at the eighth-grade level. A recent study conducted with the assistance of Texas A&M University found that migrant family heads surveyed had an average of less than one year of school.

A broad range of supportive services can be funded by NMWP: medical expenses up to $200, day care, and transportation to training, among others. However, the projects are expected to make maximum use of existing programs of all levels of government and in private nonprofit sectors. It is suggested that services to NMWP enrollees from agencies outside the NMWP should be 25 percent of NMWP funding.

The follow-up services are to include both data gathering, which is valuable for assessment of the NMWP activities, and services to former enrollees in resolving problems arising after placement.

The four program areas of NMWP include the areas where most migrants live and work throughout the year. Area I includes the demand states of the Midwest and Great Lakes area, Area II the South and Atlantic Seaboard states, and Area III Western and Rocky Mountain states. Area IV consists of

Texas, the largest supply state. (Project sites and number of enrollees in each are shown in the accompanying table).

The area with the most difficult problems is the home-base area of Texas. Human resources are underdeveloped and the economies are generally stagnant. Most of the Texas NMWP programs have emphasized public employment programs. The exception is the Cleveland, Texas, project, which is designed to be the staging area for relocation of migrants from the Rio Grande Valley to nearby areas, including Houston, Beaumont-Port Arthur-Orange, and East Texas.

A preliminary examination of the program indicates that several problems may arise with the NMWP. First, the Department of Labor has raised placement targets, which is likely to encourage creaming. Second, although the public employment programs for NMWP enrollees are probably a necessary part of any program that is to assist the most disadvantaged migratory workers, these programs are not likely to continue once NMWP funding expires. There has been little coordination of individual projects within program areas. For example, the State Migrant Review Committee (which was to consist of representatives from the Governor's planning staff, the Texas Education Agency, the Texas Employment Commission, and other involved agencies) never materialized.

An extensive evaluation of NMWP has recently been undertaken by the Urban Research Group. Approximately half of all NMWP enrollees were interviewed, and the administrative and program effectiveness was evaluated. Interestingly, preliminary results from the project indicate that 40 percent of the program participants were local seasonal farm workers rather than true interstate migrants.[6]

Other Programs

A number of other special projects for migrants should be mentioned. One of these, the Texas migrant education program, was launched in 1962. Beginning with 3,000 students in the Rio Grande Valley in 1963, this program expanded to include 55,000 students in ninety-nine districts in 1970-1971. The basic objective of the project is to meet the special education needs of migrants. Special programs to accomplish this include preschool training to prepare five-year-olds for the first grade; programs to gear the school year to the special needs of migrants; summer school and enrichment programs;

---

[6] Urban Research Group, *Evaluation of the National Migrant Worker Program* (Austin, Texas: Urban Research Group, mimeographed, 1974).

NUMBER OF ENROLLEES
IN THE NATIONAL MIGRANT WORKER PLAN, BY LOCATION,
APRIL 15, 1973

Area	Enrollees
Area I	
Muskegon, Michigan	85
Greenville/Union City, Ohio	20
Fremont, Ohio	20
South Bend, Indiana	30
Area II	
Pompano Beach, Florida	213
Lake Worth, Florida	175
Homestead, Florida	358
Rochester, New York	60
Area III	
Davis, California	
Blythe, California	
Brawley, California	
Coachella, California	115*
Brentwood, California	
Fresno, California	
Keyes, California	
Boise, Idaho	67
Blackfoot, Idaho	10
Caldwell, Idaho	13
Rupert, Idaho	
Twin Falls, Idaho	13
Ogden, Utah	31
Salt Lake City, Utah	75
Trinidad, Colorado	17
Greeley, Colorado	19
Pueblo, Colorado	18
Portland, Oregon	n.a.
Area IV	
Laredo, Texas	100
Rio Grande City, Texas	67
Corpus Christi, Texas	156
Edinburg, Texas	315
Cleveland, Texas	**

* Approximate total for California.

** Not available but funded for 275 slots for project life with an average of approximately 60 percent at one time.

Source: Department of Labor as of April 15, 1973.

provision of special materials and teachers; cooperation with other states in the migrant streams; and bilingual education.

Federal funds for migrant education are available under Title I of the Elementary and Secondary Education Act of 1965. During 1967, the first full year of operation under the "migrant amendment" to Title I, the federal government awarded $9.5 million to forty-four states; this amount rose to $37.7 million in 1968. In addition, the U.S. Office of Education has allotted funds for migrants under other titles.

Moreover, the Office of Economic Opportunity (OEO) has programs for migrants that provide day care, adult education, a compensatory education program, a high school equivalency program, and education and consulting to project directors.

The U.S. Office of Education also has funded a uniform migrant student record transfer system to facilitate the transfer of migrant student records through a computerized system with 300 terminals.

The education of migrant children remains a controversial matter. Migrants and their representatives are critical of the program, for which $97 million was appropriated the first three years. For example, the National Committee on Education of Migrant Children reported in 1971 that the program "had not dented indifference to and neglect of migrants on the part of cities and states." Moreover, our conversations with Texas education officials suggest that the migrant education project has done little other than changing schedules to gear education to the value systems and experience of migrant children. The curricula apparently are essentially the same as those given nonmigrant children, and too few of the teachers are bilingual.

Conclusions on Migrants

Considerable attention has been devoted to the problems of migrants, and the magnitude of this problem is being diminished by the steady decline in the demand for seasonal agricultural workers. However, some migrant representatives dispute the U.S. Department of Labor's figures. In any event, it probably is an exaggeration to consider migrants the most disadvantaged group in rural America. Their plight is desperate because of declining demand and because their mobile nature creates special problems for them. But many other workers in the United States, especially in the Deep South, have lower incomes and equally serious problems. Because they are in motion and therefore visible, migrants have caught public attention, although Senator Walter Mondale, chairman of the Senate Subcommittee on Migratory Labor, is correct in arguing that migrants have benefited relatively little from that attention, in spite of many programs designed to help them.[7] The nonmigrant poor black, white, and brown workers of the rural South are less visible, but their problems are at least as serious. Moreover, these workers greatly outnumber migrants.

Mexican Workers

One of the problems confronting rural workers in Texas has been competition from legal and illegal entrants from Mexico. This problem has been exacerbated in recent years by the location of plants along the Mexican side of the border to assemble goods to be sold in the United States. A special provision of the U.S. tariff code makes it possible for these goods to be shipped back into the United States tariff-free, except for the small amount of wages paid to Mexicans. These plants apparently attract many more workers to the border than can be employed there. Although little is known about the extent of this problem, many of these excess workers have joined the large numbers who have crossed the border every year either as commuters or as illegal aliens.

Commuters, generally termed "green carders" because of the original color of the resident permits, live in Mexico but work in the United States; they are technically immigrants, but they can live where they please. They are free to come and go, so long as no absence from the United States exceeds one year or they do not become unemployed for over six months. The Texas Good Neighbor Commission reported in 1970 that there were 702,000 Mexican green carders, 80 percent of whom were concentrated in Texas and California. Of these green carders, at the end of May 1969, 47,315 Mexican alien commuters were identified, 88 percent of whom worked in Texas and California (22,263 in Texas and 19,423 in California).[8] There were in addition innumerable illegal entrants; 277,377 Mexicans were apprehended and deported in 1970.

These Mexican workers create serious problems for rural workers in Texas, whose wages are depressed by their presence. Moreover, the impact of measures to improve the workers' lot is dissipated by large numbers of workers crossing the border. The chief victims of this competition from people who have American wages and Mexican living costs are Mexican Americans who compete most directly with them. As with other powerless

---

[7] *New York Times*, March 22, 1971.

[8] "Employment of 'Green Card' Aliens during Labor Disputes," statement of J. L. Hennessy during hearings before the Special Subcommittee on Labor of the Committee on Education and Labor, House of Representatives, 91st Congress, first session (Washington, D.C.: Government Printing Office, 1969), pp. 67-70.

groups, Mexican Americans have had little influence on policies to curb the numbers of commuters and illegal entrants.

STATISTICAL APPENDIX

All data in the tables, unless otherwise noted, were derived from estimates based upon a sample of approximately 50 percent of the Texas counties. Raw data from U.S. Bureau of the Census publications were assembled into a computer data bank at the Center for the Study of Human Resources, The University of Texas, Austin, Texas.

Table A-1

CHANGES IN EMPLOYMENT BY INDUSTRY IN EAST NONMETROPOLITAN TEXAS, 1960-1970

Industry	1960	1970	Change in employment	Percent change in employment
Total employment	460,049	522,139	62,090	13.5
Agriculture, forestry, and fisheries	79,043	42,151	– 36,892	– 46.7
Mining	15,117	10,688	– 4,429	– 29.3
Construction	37,183	42,995	5,812	15.6
Manufacturing	74,043	93,501	19,458	26.3
Durable goods	44,010	64,264	20,254	46.0
Furniture and lumber	12,926	17,114	4,188	32.4
Metal industries	7,535	15,971	8,436	119.6
Machinery, excluding electrical	4,558	8,184	3,626	79.5
Electrical machinery	1,002	4,289	3,287	328.0
Transport equipment	12,221	8,909	– 3,312	– 27.1
Other durable goods	5,768	9,797	4,029	69.8
Nondurable goods	30,033	29,237	– 796	– 2.7
Food	8,392	7,656	– 736	– 8.7
Textiles and apparel	7,921	10,511	2,590	32.7
Printing and publishing	3,608	4,232	624	17.3
Chemicals	3,617	5,401	1,784	49.3
Other nondurable	6,495	1,437	– 5,058	– 77.9
Railroads	7,989	6,444	– 1,545	– 19.3
Trucking and warehousing	5,826	6,154	328	5.6
Other transport	5,057	5,316	259	5.1
Communications	4,064	5,579	1,515	37.3
Utilities and sanitary service	7,798	10,009	2,211	28.3
Wholesale trade	10,973	14,249	3,276	29.9
Food, bakery, and dairy stores	15,557	14,789	– 768	– 4.9
Eating and drinking	13,982	15,864	1,882	13.5
Other retail trade	51,083	61,711	10,628	20.8
Finance, insurance, and real estate	11,865	16,353	4,488	37.8

Table A-1 (Continued)

Industry	1960	1970	Change in employment	Percent change in employment
Business service and repair	9,951	11,500	1,549	15.6
Private household service	24,329	15,451	– 8,878	– 36.5
Other personal service	17,322	20,396	3,074	17.8
Entertainment and recreation	2,358	3,098	740	31.4
Hospital and health services	12,383	28,837	16,454	132.9
Education (all)	29,120	46,591	17,471	60.0
Welfare, religious and nonprofit	5,787	6,539	752	13.0
Legal, engineering, and other	6,640	8,502	1,862	28.0
Public administration	17,771	25,423	7,652	43.1

Table A-2

CHANGES IN EMPLOYMENT BY INDUSTRY IN SOUTHWEST NONMETROPOLITAN TEXAS, 1960-1970

Industry	1960	1970	Change in employment	Percent change in employment
Total employment	284,865	273,180	– 11,685	– 4.1
Agriculture, forestry, and fisheries	60,901	37,679	– 23,222	– 38.1
Mining	22,232	19,037	– 3,195	– 14.4
Construction	23,975	23,453	– 522	– 2.2
Manufacturing	23,219	25,520	2,301	9.9
Durable goods	5,389	7,021	1,632	30.3
Furniture and lumber	487	782	295	60.6
Metal industries	2,818	3,041	223	7.9
Machinery, excluding electrical	643	680	37	5.8
Electrical machinery	55	481	426	774.6

Table A-2 (Continued)

Industry	1960	1970	Change in employment	Percent change in employment
Transport equipment	477	718	241	50.5
Other durable goods	909	2,101	1,192	131.1
Nondurable goods	17,830	17,717	– 113	– 0.6
Food	4,494	3,630	– 864	– 19.2
Textiles and apparel	5,265	5,712	447	8.5
Printing and publishing	1,379	1,474	95	6.9
Chemicals	1,689	2,436	747	44.2
Other nondurable	5,003	4,465	– 538	– 10.8
Railroads	2,759	1,413	– 1,346	– 48.8
Trucking and warehousing	4,181	3,537	– 644	– 15.4
Other transport	2,889	2,004	– 885	– 29.6
Communications	2,743	2,533	– 210	– 7.7
Utilities and sanitary service	5,643	6,589	946	16.8
Wholesale trade	8,363	7,453	– 910	– 10.9
Food, bakery, and dairy stores	9,141	8,247	– 894	– 9.8
Eating and drinking	10,835	9,478	– 1,357	– 12.5
Other retail trade	31,588	32,241	653	2.1
Finance, insurance, and real estate	6,252	8,122	1,870	29.9
Business services and repair	6,455	6,746	291	4.5
Private household services	12,434	8,097	– 4,337	– 34.9
Other personal services	9,357	10,016	659	7.0
Entertainment and recreation	1,974	1,951	– 23	– 1.2
Hospital and health services	5,435	12,505	7,070	130.1
Education (all)	15,406	23,360	7,954	51.6
Welfare, religious and nonprofit	2,740	3,370	630	22.9
Legal, engineering, and other	3,817	5,409	1,592	41.7
Public administration	12,522	14,421	1,899	15.1

Table A-3

CHANGES IN EMPLOYMENT BY INDUSTRY IN NORTHWEST NONMETROPOLITAN TEXAS, 1960-1970

Industry	1960	1970	Change in employment	Percent change in employment
Total employment	236,459	214,275	– 22,184	– 9.4
Agriculture, forestry, and fisheries	58,685	42,933	– 15,752	– 26.8
Mining	13,853	9,869	– 4,084	– 29.5
Construction	17,953	14,694	– 3,259	– 18.2
Manufacturing	21,183	23,395	2,212	10.4
Durable goods	5,257	6,806	1,549	29.5
Furniture and lumber	259	612	353	136.3
Metal industries	522	942	420	80.5
Machinery, excluding electrical	1,927	2,189	262	13.6
Electrical machinery	41	251	210	512.2
Transport equipment	313	899	586	187.2
Other durable goods	2,195	1,913	– 282	– 12.9
Nondurable goods	15,926	16,589	663	4.2
Food	2,790	2,505	– 285	– 10.2
Textile and apparel	1,653	5,510	3,857	233.3
Printing and publishing	1,925	1,571	– 354	– 18.4
Chemicals	4,566	2,476	– 2,090	– 45.8
Other nondurable	4,992	4,527	– 465	– 9.3
Railroads	2,768	1,607	– 1,161	– 41.9
Trucking and warehousing	3,965	3,030	– 935	– 23.6
Other transport	1,756	1,484	– 272	– 15.5
Communications	2,630	2,596	– 34	– 1.3
Utilities and sanitary service	4,671	4,711	40	0.8
Wholesale trade	7,294	6,617	– 677	– 9.3
Food, bakery, and dairy stores	6,503	5,312	– 1,191	– 18.3
Eating and drinking	7,149	6,747	– 402	– 5.6
Other retail trade	26,834	26,914	80	0.3
Finance, insurance, and real estate	5,709	6,382	673	11.8

Table A-3 (Continued)

Industry	1960	1970	Change in employment	Percent change in employment
Business services and repairs	5,611	5,313	– 298	– 5.3
Private household services	7,644	4,750	– 2,894	– 37.9
Other personal services	8,614	7,855	– 759	– 8.8
Entertainment and recreation	1,132	964	– 168	– 14.8
Hospitals and health services	3,797	10,615	6,818	179.6
Education (all)	12,635	15,168	2,533	20.0
Welfare, religious and nonprofit	3,334	2,991	– 343	– 10.3
Legal engineering and others	3,505	3,037	– 468	– 13.4
Public administration	8,249	7,295	– 954	– 11.6

Table A-4

THE IMPACT OF GROWTH ON HUMAN RESOURCE DEVELOPMENT VARIABLES: MULTIPLE REGRESSION RESULTS

Independent variables[1]	Family income 1970	Poverty 1970	Working poor 1970	Reduction in nonworker status 1965-1970	Participation rate 1970	Enrollment rate 1970
Δ Durable goods 1960-1970	–	–*	–	–	–	–
Δ Nondurable goods 1960-1970	–	+*	+**	–	–	+
Δ Total employment 1960-1970	+*	–	–*	+	+	+
Industrial structure, male	+***	–***	–***	–*	+***	+
Industrial structure, female	–***	+***	+***	–*	–*	–*
Change in industrial structure, male, 1960-1970	–**	+***	+***	+*	–***	+
Wage level, 1970	+***	–***	–***	+*	–***	+**
Percent black, 1970	–	+***	+	–***	–***	+
Southwest region	–	+	+	–	+***	–*
Summary statistics						
R^2	41.85%	48.14%	46.06%	18.49%	47.31%	20.39%
F (9, 102)	8.15	10.52	9.68	2.57	10.17	2.90

1 See explanation of independent variables, following.
–, + Sign of the regression coefficients.
*** Significant at the .01 level.
** Significant at the .05 level.
* Significant at the .10 level.

Variables Used in the Regression Analysis

Family income, 1970 = median family income, by county, 1970.
Poverty, 1970 = percent of families in poverty, by county, 1970.
Working poor, 1970 = proportion of the male, civilian labor force who are working but still are in poverty, by county, 1970.
Reduction in nonworker status, 1970 = proportion of nonworking males in 1965 who became workers in 1970, by county, 1970 (males, thirty to forty-nine years of age, 1970).
Participation rate, 1970 = male participation rate, by county, 1970.
Enrollment rate, 1970 = percent of those sixteen and seventeen years old who were enrolled in school, by county, 1970.
Δ*Durable goods, 1960-1970* = per capita change in durable goods employment, by county, 1960-1970.
Δ*Nondurable goods, 1960-1970* = per capita change in nondurable goods employment, by county, 1960-1970.
Δ*Total employment, 1960-1970* = percentage rate of change in total employment, by county, 1960-1970.
Industrial structure, male = index of occupationally expected earnings for male nonagricultural employment, by county, 1970.
Industrial structure, female = index of occupationally expected earnings for female nonagricultural employment, by county, 1970.
Change in industrial structure, male, 1960-1970 = change in the index of occupationally expected earnings for male nonagricultural employment, by county, 1960-1970.
Wage level, 1970 = index of male wages after controlling for the occupational structure, by county, 1970.
Percent black, 1970 = percent of the 1970 population that was black.
Southwest region = 1, 0 dummy variable, 1 indicating the county is in the Southwest, 0 otherwise.
Source: All variables were derived from 1960 and 1970 U.S. Census publications.

Table A-5

OCCUPATIONAL CHANGES FOR MALES
IN EAST NONMETROPOLITAN TEXAS, 1960-1970, 1970-1980

Occupation	1960	1970	Change in employment, 1960-1970	Percent change in employment, 1960-1970	Forecasted change in employment, 1970-1980
Total employed	331,670	336,884	5,214	1.6	41,333
Professional and technical	23,074	30,591	7,517	32.6	9,973
Farmers and farm managers	46,318	21,689	– 24,629	– 53.2	– 5,769
Managers	34,483	36,706	2,223	6.4	2,349
Clerical	14,661	18,348	3,687	25.2	4,624
Sales	18,132	19,579	1,447	8.0	1,566
Craft workers	60,572	75,961	15,389	25.4	19,294
Operatives	64,240	70,770	6,530	10.2	7,219
Private household	2,510	419	– 2,091	– 83.3	– 349
Service workers	16,829	22,689	5,860	34.8	7,896
Farm laborers	20,821	13,590	– 7,231	– 34.7	– 2,365
Laborers, nonfarm	30,058	26,541	– 3,517	– 11.7	– 3,105

Table A-6

OCCUPATIONAL CHANGES FOR FEMALES
IN EAST NONMETROPOLITAN TEXAS, 1960-1970, 1970-1980

Occupation	1960	1970	Change in employment, 1960-1970	Percent change in employment, 1960-1970	Forecasted change in employment, 1970-1980
Total employed	139,708	185,872	46,164	33.0	90,690
Professional and technical	21,700	27,840	6,140	28.3	7,879
Farmers and farm managers	2,892	1,173	– 1,719	– 59.4	– 348
Managers	6,723	7,666	943	14.0	1,073
Clerical	28,766	49,432	20,666	71.8	35,492
Sales	12,932	13,949	1,017	7.9	1,102
Craft workers	1,718	3,495	1,777	103.4	3,614
Operatives	14,791	23,284	8,493	57.4	13,365
Private household	20,904	14,636	– 6,268	– 30.0	– 4,391
Service workers	23,302	40,055	16,753	71.9	28,800
Farm laborers	5,115	1,918	– 3,197	– 62.5	– 599
Laborers, nonfarm	824	2,423	1,599	194.1	4,703

Table A-7

OCCUPATIONAL CHANGES FOR MALES IN SOUTHWEST NONMETROPOLITAN TEXAS, 1960-1970, 1970-1980

Occupation	1960	1970	Change in employment, 1960-1970	Percent change in employment, 1960-1970	Forecasted change in employment, 1970-1980
Total employed	206,882	180,293	− 26,589	− 12.9	− 7,329
Professional and technical	13,152	10,757	− 2,395	− 18.2	− 1,958
Farmers and farm managers	27,934	14,169	− 13,765	− 49.3	− 3,500
Managers	22,334	18,236	− 4,098	− 18.4	− 3,355
Clerical	7,954	8,751	797	10.0	875
Sales	8,534	9,449	915	10.7	1,011
Craft workers	34,934	36,321	1,387	4.0	1,453
Operatives	41,711	37,263	− 4,448	− 10.7	− 3,987
Private household	443	391	− 52	− 11.6	− 45
Service workers	8,480	12,411	3,931	46.4	5,759
Farm laborers	24,971	16,072	− 8,899	− 35.6	− 2,861
Laborers, nonfarm	16,435	15,672	− 763	− 4.6	− 721

Table A-8

OCCUPATIONAL CHANGES FOR FEMALES IN SOUTHWEST NONMETROPOLITAN TEXAS, 1960-1970, 1970-1980

Occupation	1960	1970	Change in employment, 1960-1970	Percent change in employment, 1960-1970	Forecasted change in employment, 1970-1980
Total employed	71,417	93,648	22,231	31.1	49,382
Professional and technical	10,384	18,337	7,953	76.6	14,046
Farmers and farm managers	1,276	890	− 386	− 30.3	− 135
Managers	4,554	4,931	377	8.3	409
Clerical	16,916	24,753	7,837	46.3	11,461
Sales	6,320	6,516	196	3.1	202
Craft workers	413	2,641	2,228	539.5	14,248
Operatives	5,691	7,007	1,316	23.1	1,619
Private household	10,126	7,377	− 2,749	− 27.2	− 2,007
Service workers	13,101	18,897	5,796	44.2	8,352
Farm laborers	2,181	1,228	− 953	− 43.7	− 269
Laborers, nonfarm	454	1,071	617	135.9	1,455

Table A-9

OCCUPATIONAL CHANGES FOR MALES IN NORTHWEST NONMETROPOLITAN TEXAS, 1960-1970, 1970-1980

Occupation	1960	1970	Change in employment, 1960-1970	Percent change in employment, 1960-1970	Forecasted change in employment, 1970-1980
Total employed	174,970	144,171	−30,799	−17.6	−17,626
Professional and technical	11,114	10,801	−313	−2.8	−302
Farmers and farm managers	35,244	22,047	−13,197	−37.4	−4,123
Managers	19,703	14,958	−4,745	−24.1	−3,605
Clerical	6,837	6,062	−775	−11.3	−685
Sales	7,466	7,452	−14	−0.2	−14
Craft workers	30,555	27,413	−3,142	−10.3	−2,824
Operatives	31,294	24,274	7,020	−22.4	−5,437
Private household	122	70	−52	−42.6	−30
Service workers	5,859	6,966	1,107	18.9	1,317
Farm laborers	16,554	15,558	−996	−6.0	−467
Laborers, nonfarm	10,220	8,467	−1,753	−17.2	−1,456

Table A-10

OCCUPATIONAL CHANGES FOR FEMALES IN NORTHWEST NONMETROPOLITAN TEXAS, 1960-1970, 1970-1980

Occupation	1960	1970	Change in employment, 1960-1970	Percent change in employment, 1960-1970	Forecasted change in employment, 1970-1980
Total employed	56,918	68,745	11,827	20.8	18,378
Professional and technical	8,365	10,438	2,073	24.8	2,589
Farmers and farm managers	633	608	−25	−4.0	−12
Managers	3,331	3,072	−259	−7.8	−240
Clerical	13,915	18,874	4,959	35.6	6,719
Sales	5,709	5,610	−99	−1.7	−95
Craft workers	557	1,326	769	138.1	1,831
Operatives	5,376	6,806	1,430	26.6	1,810
Private household	6,246	4,296	−1,950	−31.2	−1,340
Service workers	11,696	16,404	4,708	40.3	6,611
Farm laborers	827	780	−47	−5.7	−22
Laborers, nonfarm	265	529	264	99.6	527